Option for the Poor

Berkeley Lecture Series 1

Option for the Poor

The Basic Principle of Liberation Theology in the Light of the Bible

by

Norbert F. Lohfink, S.J.

Translated by Linda M. Maloney, Ph.D.
Edited by Duane L. Christensen

BIBAL Press
Publishing agency of BIBAL Corporation
The Berkeley Institute of Biblical Archaeology & Literature

Option for the Poor
The Basic Principle of Liberation Theology in the Light of the Bible

Copyright © 1987 by BIBAL Press
Second Edition, 1995

The Bailey Lectures
March 31 – April 2, 1986

Library of Congress Cataloging-in-Publication Data

Lohfink, Norbert.
    Option for the poor : the basic principle of liberation theology in the light of the Bible / by Norbert Lohfink ; translated by Linda M. Maloney ; edited by Duane L. Christensen. — 2nd ed.
        p.   cm. — (Berkeley lecture series ; 1)
    ISBN 0-941037-38-X
    1. Poverty in the Bible. 2. Church work with the poor—Catholic Church. 3. Liberation theology. 4. Catholic Church—Doctrines. 5. Catholic Church—Membership.   I. Title. II. Series.
BS680.P47L64 1995
261.8'325—dc20   95-25305
                                                                   CIP

Published by BIBAL Press
P.O. Box 821653
N. Richland Hills, TX 76182

Printed in the U.S.A.

Contents

Editor's Foreword

In his initial lecture at the American Baptist Seminary of the West on March 31, 1986 Professor Lohfink made the following statement:

> You have invited me to give this year's Bailey Lectures. I was honored to receive this invitation, and I was happy to accept it, out of a longstanding love for Berkeley and the pleasure I have in being able to visit my friend and colleague in Deuteronomy research, Dr. Duane Christensen. And it was amazing how quickly I was able to reach an agreement with Dr. William Malcomson, the Vice President of the American Baptist Seminary of the West and Dean of Academic Affairs, that this year's topic should be: "God and the Poor According to the Bible."

As things turned out the lecture series was a resounding success, particularly in regards to the stimulating discussion sessions at the conclusion of each of the three presentations. The substance of the lectures are presented here in substantially the form in which they were delivered. It is a pity that we cannot reproduce what happened in the interchange between audience and speaker.

It is most fitting that this particular volume is the initial publication of BIBAL Press, the publishing agency of the Berkeley Institute of Biblical Archaeology and Literature (BIBAL) has been established to fund and administer projects, including publication, in the area of biblical studies, including archaeology. The institute is a nonprofit corporation whose projects include research, excavation, teaching, and publication. Professor Lohfink's *Option for the Poor* is a stimulating study of a timely issue, which demonstrates the best in exegetical method on the part of one who has mastered the biblical text and knows how to relate that text to the central issues of today.

The following comments testify to the worth of this book:

"The only major study by a biblical scholar of one of the most important and most controversial phrases in contemporary theology and church life. The 'option for the poor' may be as controversial and important for our generation as was 'justification by faith' for previous ones. This study, by an internationally respected Old Testament scholar, is indispensable for engaging its roots in the Bible and its contemporary challenge."

Rev. John R. Donahue, S.J.
Professor of New Testament
Jesuit School of Theology and Graduate Theological Union

"These lectures present a moving and scholarly account of the biblical notion of God's love for the poor. After showing that this concept was prominent among Israel's neighbors, Lohfink examines its unique meaning in the Old and New Testaments, and its affinity to and difference from liberation theology. These lectures made me see things in a new way."

John Dillenberger
Professor Emeritus
Graduate Theological Union

"Father Norbert F. Lohfink's Option for the Poor makes great reading. It calls attention to important, neglected aspects of biblical social teaching. It does so by focusing on major, sublime texts, so the reader feels invited rather than pressured. And it is imbued with a generous spirit, open to pre-Christian attainments both Jewish and pagan. This slim volume should engender a prolonged and fruitful discussion."

David Daube
Professor Emeritus
School of Law (Boalt Hall), University of California, Berkeley

"I find his ideas and his discussion of them to be most convincing
. . . they are strongly put, yet simply. I find it a very readable book
which many churches might use in adult and youth discussions. And
certainly clergy would find it a very fine way to get into the entire
field as so few clergy have as yet. This is a very exciting book for me
. . . It gives me my first soundly grounded biblical basis to understand
the third world . . . Lohfink has such great energy, mild humor,
informality and common sense plus obvious scholarship . . . He must
be a fine person."

Miles Clark
Retired author and publisher

"Professor Lohfink has set a high standard to emulate. We hope
this is the first of a long series of significant publications on the part
of BIBAL Press."

Duane L. Christensen, Director
Berkeley Institute of Biblical Archaeology and Literature

John W. Bailey
and the Bailey Lectures

The Bailey Lectures at the American Baptist Seminary of the West are given annually to honor a distinguished New Testament scholar, Professor John W. Bailey. Dr. Bailey taught at the seminary for thirty-two years, was professor of New Testament Interpretation, and in retirement became professor emeritus.

Dr. Bailey was born in 1873 in Indiana and died in Berkeley at the age of ninety-six on June 6, 1969. He graduated from Franklin College in 1898. He earned his B.D. in 1901 and his Ph.D. magna cum laude in 1904 from the University of Chicago. He served pastorates in Illinois, Wisconsin, and Iowa, and then became president of Central College in Pella, Iowa. Later he was president of Colorado Woman's College in Denver.

While Dr. Bailey taught in Berkeley, the seminary was known as the Berkeley Baptist Divinity School. He authored six books in the biblical field and was a contributor to The Interpreter's Bible (on Thessalonians). In retirement, he continued to teach for nine years at the seminary, and served as an interim pastor, author, and book reviewer.

For more than thirty years, Dr. Bailey taught an adult Bible class at the First Baptist Church of Berkeley. That class established a fund which became the financial resource for the Bailey Lectures. When Louise Bailey died, additional gifts in her memory strengthened the Bailey Lecture Fund.

My predecessor, the late President Emeritus Sandford Fleming, spoke appreciatively of Dr. Bailey's "profound scholarship," and said that he gave "his students an understanding and appreciation which brought personal enrichment and prepared them to preach and teach (the Bible) intelligently and persuasively."

How appropriate that our major lecture series should be named for John Bailey! Through the years, outstanding Christian scholars have been invited to present the lectures. Among them have been Herman Waetjen, Walter Brueggemann, Ross Snyder, Georg Braulik, Dale Moody, Robert Guelich, and Barrie White.

Dr. Norbert Lohfink's stimulating and thought-provoking lectures in March, 1986 continued a rich tradition of serious scholarship and application to life situations. We are delighted that this fine series, which stirred and challenged us when given publicly at the seminary, will now be available to evoke reflection and, I pray, action by a widening circle of friends and readers.

Wesley H. Brown
President, American Baptist Seminary of the West (1987)

Norbert F. Lohfink, S.J.

The author of this volume has long been known in professional circles worldwide, but it has only been the translation of several of his German works into English, his visiting professor role in Berkeley, and various U.S. public lectures that have introduced him to a wider American audience.

Who's Who in Biblical Studies devotes considerable space to his academic achievements. His degrees: Licentiate in Philosophy from Munich in 1957, Licentiate in Theology from Frankfurt in 1957, and Doctorate in Biblical Studies from the Pontifical Biblical Institute in Rome in 1963. His teaching career has extended broadly—from Munich to Frankfurt, to the Pontifical Biblical Institute in Rome, and westward to a stint as visiting professor at the Jesuit School of Theology in Berkeley.

His publications range from nineteen volumes to numerous articles and reviews. Of significance as well has been his service as editor for some years of the Stuttgarter Bibelstudien and Biblica.

In addition to his academic activities, for many years Professor Lohfink has associated himself with the "Integrierte Gemeinde," a group of some five hundred Munich Christians concerned with biblical, liturgical, and community renewal.

The lengthy and distinguished academic career of Professor Lohfink, plus many years of pastoral ministry as well, render him an ideal choice to undertake the topic of the current volume. He has clearly delineated the profound relevance of the biblical text for one of the most vibrant issues of our day.

John E. Huesman, S.J.
Jesuit School of Theology, Berkeley

---> 1 >≈≈-

Horizons
God and the Poor in the Ancient Near East

What are the presuppositions, theological and historical, of the
biblical talk of God's love for the poor?

Modern science and technology make it possible to transform
the riches of God's creation into the still greater riches of a world of
human design. The modern advantages of transportation and com-
munication allow us to distribute this wealth rapidly and justly
throughout the world. And yet, the contrary is what happens. The
creation is being exhausted and losing its bright and colorful appearance. The differences between North and South, upper and lower,
rich and poor increase from day to day. This is a scandal. We
Christians are aware of it. We ourselves are actors in the drama, in
one way or another. Are we alarmed? If we are, how do we react?

There is, thank God, a worldwide alarm in our day among
Christians. And there is a reaction which, in one of the earth's regions
most affected by the situation, the Latin American continent, has been
condensed especially in the motto: "option of the Church for the
poor." Theology is also involved. The "theology of liberation"
understands itself as an ongoing reflection on the ecclesial-social
process that is developing in light of the option for the poor.

One of the most important tasks of a theology that concerns
itself with the option for the poor is constantly to check what
Christians today are doing by comparison with the Word of God in
sacred Scripture. Now, the well-known names in liberation theology
[I will mention only one, that of Gustavo Gutiérrez, as representative]
are those of practitioners of systematic theology. Undoubtedly they
have developed a much more spontaneous and direct relationship

1

with the Bible than systematic theology has ever had in Europe or
North America in recent centuries. That much should be clearly
established. On the other hand we have to add that in the matter of
the option of the churches for the poor, the Bible has not yet been
called upon to say all that it has to say.

The concern I find in America for "God and the Poor According
to the Bible" is heartening to me. To discover this commonality of
interest was in itself a pleasure. For in a sense there are great distances
that divide us. I live in faraway Europe, I am a Catholic and a member
of the Society of Jesus. But the subject of the poor, and the spontaneous turn to the Bible—these two things evidently unite us beyond
all our differences.

Every third year, I teach for several months at the Pontifical
Biblical Institute in Rome. On one such occasion, two years ago, I
was requested by the newly-elected General Superior of my Order,
Father Peter-Hans Kolvenbach, to sum up for him in a memorandum
what the Bible had to say about the "option for the poor." I wrote it,
and when he had read through it he asked me to expand it into a
book. I have been working on that book since then, together with my
brother, who is Professor of New Testament in Tübingen. The title
of the book will probably be: *God on the Side of the Poor: Biblical
Investigations in Liberation Theology* . I am presenting here some
thoughts that have suggested themselves in the course of that larger
work.

Of course it would be quite impossible to exhaust the subject of
"God and the Poor" in the whole Bible in one small book. It is such
a central theme in the Bible that it is connected to everything and
appears in every possible context. The authors of the first draft of the
U.S. Catholic bishops' pastoral letter "On Catholic Social Teaching
and the U.S. Economy" have, in my opinion, fallen victims to this
situation, and the same could probably be said of the authors of the
second draft. In their biblical exposition, praiseworthy for the
breadth of its concept, they seem to find themselves rather at sea, and
one is often not at all sure what course they are sailing. I will attempt,
on the contrary, only to select several precisely defined questions
which the Bible forces us to ask in face of the contrast between poor

and rich in our world. Many other important matters will not enter the discussion. Please do not be surprised, then, that I do not, for example, go very deeply into the social critique of Israel's prophets. It is not that I consider it unimportant. But it is more important that we take up some questions that are less often posed in connection with the theology of liberation.

The first question is that of presuppositions. What does the Bible presuppose, as a matter of course, when it asserts that God shows a special love and attention to the poor? The question can be asked in terms of biblical theology: What kind of creation does God will—a rich or an impoverished creation? But the question of presuppositions can also be posed in historical terms: What was the attitude to the poor and to poverty of the surrounding society in which Israel, the people of God, lived and grew? This twofold question about the presuppositions of the biblical talk of God's inclination to the poor is not asked often enough today. The pastoral letter I have just mentioned, for example, emphasizes much too one-sidedly that the Bible regards riches as a danger. It has nothing to say about the treatment of the poor in Israel's surroundings and therefore makes, to mention one example, the easily-refuted statement that concern for widows and orphans was a distinctive feature of the Bible.

The second question concerns the distinctive character of the Bible. What is it that is new and different when the God of Israel concerns himself with the poor, in contrast to what the other societies in the world do? We need to discuss this question especially on the basis of the theme of Israel's being led out of Egypt.

The third question is: What did it really mean when Jesus designated the gospel as a "gospel for the poor?" This question has to be answered primarily on the basis of the Old Testament, and especially from the book of Isaiah.

All that by way of preview. And now, *medias in res* .

The Biblical-Theological Horizon of the Biblical Declaration of God's Special Concern for the Poor.

In order not to be too long-winded, I will simply propose five theses and try to make a few remarks on each of them.

God Is Interested in the Here and Now

That God's actions in the Old Testament are entirely directed to this world needs no proof. But in many Christian circles, it is common to set the New Testament over against the Old and to see there a new kind of message having to do with another world. The bourgeois concept of religion has made good use of this in modern times to remove the non-religious sectors of society from any direction motivated by faith. Marxist critique of religion then reproaches Christianity for offering this otherworldly consolation. We can thus reduce the question for the moment to this: What about this supposed pure otherworldliness of the New Testament message?

In the Lord's Prayer we read: "Hallowed be Thy name. Thy kingdom come. Thy will be done" (Matt 6:9-10). All three petitions are concerned with God's action, for the passives are all *passiva divina*. God's action for which we are to pray is, however, thought of as action here and now. The third petition reads in full: "Thy will be done on earth as it is in heaven." The earth is the place where God acts. The address "Our Father in heaven" and the extension of the third petition "on earth as it is in heaven" are connected by the key word "heaven" and frame all three petitions. The closing words "on earth as it is in heaven" bring the opening location "in heaven" to its goal. God is addressed in heaven, but what is asked for is to happen on earth. There is, then, only one correct interpretation of the first half of the Lord's Prayer: God is to hallow his name in *this* world, his will is something which happens in *this* history. His rule is coming, since Jesus, in *this* world.

What I am saying is not meant to cast doubt on the central place of the resurrection, of Jesus and of all the dead, in the New Testament confession. It remains central, even though the hope for a resurrection of the dead had gained significance in Israel only toward the end of the Old Testament period. But the hope of resurrection is in the New Testament, as it already had been in the Old Testament, intimately bound up with the hope for the accomplishment of God's will in this world.

In the Old Testament, this first appears in full clarity in the writings of the Maccabean period, especially in the book of Daniel. The particular hope expressed in Daniel is for the rule of the Son of Man who is to come, a rule which signifies the victory of the true divine sovereignty in our history (cf. especially Daniel 7). When it comes, even the dead will rise, for the just among them are to share in that for which they lived and perhaps even died as martyrs (Daniel 12). The resurrection of the dead belongs therefore, according to Daniel, to the beginning of the reign of God in our history.

The conviction of the apostle Paul, as we encounter it in the Acts of the Apostles, was that the resurrection is so closely connected to the beginning of God's rule in history that one can turn the question around and conclude from the fact that the resurrection of the dead has begun in Jesus of Nazareth that the eschatological reign of God has begun in history. Paul, when asked what he really intends, can answer: "It is because of the hope of Israel that I am bound with this chain" (Acts 28:20). This formulation includes everything that Israel hoped and expected. Acts summarizes it as the witness to the reign of God that has come through Jesus Christ (Acts 28:23, 31). But at the same time it can be characterized as the resurrection of the dead (Acts 23:6; 24:15; 26:6-8). In these texts, the meaning is not that Paul is preaching the general belief that sometime, somewhere the dead will rise; but that he is declaring that the expected resurrection of the dead has begun in Jesus and consequently everything else that God has promised has also begun. The burden of his preaching is that Jesus is "the first to rise from the dead" (Acts 26:23). In that *one* has risen from the dead, the raising of the dead as such has begun. And so the end-time has arrived, when the reign of God is to be accom - plished, starting with Jesus, in this world.

This is not a special notion of Paul nor of the author of Acts. It is, instead, the core of the apostolical preaching from the very beginning. Acts formulates it thus, referring to the very first weeks of the early Jerusalem community: "With great power the apostles gave their testimony to the resurrection of the Lord Jesus" (Acts 4:33). They were able to do this, as the verse continues, because it was a fact that "great grace was upon all (believers)." The "great grace" is the eschatological grace of God that had begun with the pouring out of the Spirit as promised by the prophets and that now was expressing itself in the completely altered life of the community, as depicted in the surrounding verses (Acts 4:32-35). Central to this report on the community is the statement: "There was not a needy person among them" (Acts 4:34). As I have said, all this is here, on this earth, in this history.

We are accustomed to think of the message of the resurrection, which we rightly regard as the principal article of Christian proclamation, as directed to another world. For the Bible does indeed refer to an event that leads into another world, but at the same time it is an announcement of a decisive change in this world. In the Bible there is really no basic opposition between "this world" and "another world." The real chasm gapes between the old and the new eon. The leap from one to the other happens in baptism. In this is the tremendous importance of baptism. The new eon has a this-worldly dimension.

God Is Interested in Material Things

If God's reign begins already in this world, he does not want any unworldly people in it. In the Bible, there is no mention of methods by which the spirit can be released from matter in order to become unworldly. We can presume with a good measure of certainty that Israel also had command of what we today call the techniques of meditation. But there is nothing to suggest that these were used to release oneself from the influence of the body. These techniques are in fact so irrelevant to everything about which the Bible speaks that they are nowhere even mentioned.

When God delivers his people, he leads them into a "land flowing with milk and honey" (Exod 3:8). It is a "magnificent land," a land "of brooks of water, of fountains and springs, a land of wheat and barley, of vines and fig trees and pomegranates, a land of olive trees and honey, a land in which you will eat bread without scarcity, in which you will lack nothing," where you can "eat and be full" (Deut 8:7-10).

At the same time, God promises the people that he delivers health of body: "I will put none of the diseases upon you which I put upon the Egyptians, for I am Yahweh your healer" (Exod 15:26).

This worldliness is in no way transposed into unworldliness in the New Testament. It does not become, as is often said, an image of "inner" gifts. Jesus, the Messiah, travels through the country healing the sick. He gives food to the hungry crowds and at a wedding he changes water into wine.

The question of the historicity of these stories which exegetes discuss—in John 2, for example—need not detain us here. It is enough that the evangelists represent and interpret Jesus in this way. Quite apart from the fact that this interpretation rests on concrete experiences with Jesus, it is at all events relevant for the question of the worldliness of the New Testament.

Among the few bits of information that Acts gives us on the first Christian community in Jerusalem are the descriptions of how these people dealt with worldly goods, how they saw to it that everyone ate well and that there were no "needy persons" among them (Acts 4:34). It is striking how much space in these reports is taken up with material things.

God Is Interested in Society

Every kind of bourgeois restriction of the religious sphere to the individual is also unknown to the Bible. Obviously it is always the individual heart that believes or does not believe, that is good or evil. But faith and goodness are realized in connection with God's "people." Even exegetes seldom take account of the fact that in the central

commandment to love, it is not the individual, but the people as such
that is being exhorted: "Hear, O *Israel!* Yahweh our God, Yahweh is
one. Therefore you (= Israel) shall love Yahweh your God with all
your heart, and with all your soul, and with all your might" (Deut
6:4-5).

That is, God does not deliver individuals, but a people. He
constitutes this people by giving them a cult, that is, a common
celebration; and a Torah, a social order—both of these on Sinai, that
is, (in the logic of the biblical redactors) before the entry into the
"land." The constitution of community is therefore even more central
than all the material plenty.

The eschatological promises of the prophets are directed to the
newly rebuilt "Zion," the city as symbol of the well-ordered human
society. Beginning with Deutero-Isaiah, there is expectation of a
future "reign of God." That, too, is a concept that indicates a new
society. In the book of Daniel, the reign of God replaces the old world
empires. Even the "Son of Man" is, according to the initial idea in
Daniel, first of all an image of anticipation for the eschatological
society. After the four beasts coming from the sea of social chaos—the
societies which have reigned until this time—there appears in the
vision a human being. Now, at last, a human society enters the world.

Jesus' message is that the reign of God is coming now. His
Sermon on the Mount, as Matthew presents it, transposes the old
Torah of Israel into its perfected, messianic form.

After Jesus' resurrection there arose communities which are the
"ekklesia," the assembly of the people of God—another social con-
ception. By far the largest part of the New Testament consists of
letters to "church communities"; and the second sections of the
letters, which we often neglect, are made up of regulations for the
common life. Even the Apocalypse ends with the vision of the
heavenly city coming down to earth, fulfillment of human longing
for the true society.

God Is Interested in Plenitude and Riches

This aspect of biblical theology must be especially emphasized in the context of a discussion concerning the "poor."

In my church, at least, the expression "Church of the poor" is on every tongue at the present time. It is not biblical. We find it in the Dead Sea scrolls (4Qp Ps 37:2,9 and 3,10). It is therefore all the more astonishing that it is not in the New Testament. In our century, it apparently comes from the French spirituality of poverty dating from the war years and the period immediately after. In Albert Gelin's influential book, *Les Pauvres de Yahvé* (The Poor of Yahweh), it is already present as a matter of course. Today it is by no means only the Church in Latin America that talks of a "Church of the poor." At least when the expression is used in European countries, one can often hear an echo of something like criticism of a good and happy life as such. "Church of the poor"—among us that frequently sounds almost as if the Church ought to be essentially some sort of zone for wretchedness, simplicity, narrowness of life, restriction of the world's reality, a kind of place in the world where no one hopes to rise higher and each is content with little in all areas of life. Among our students, the talk of the "simple life" is usually not far distant. But is that more than a kind of romanticism of upper middle class children who never experienced what poverty really is?

There can, of course, be a lofty ethic in this talk of the "Church of the poor," especially when it is a protest reaction against worship of self-advancement, self-importance, mammoth industry, ruthless exploitation of the earth, accumulation of power by industry, and international economic concentration. So far as that is the case, I have nothing to say against it. But sometimes the call for a "Church of the poor" sounds like an ideology prepared for those who have not quite made it, for whom the Church's message should serve to justify and sacralize their situation. Such an echo would be thoroughly unbiblical.

God is the creator. He has created an abundant fullness of reality. He wills a world of wealth and plenty, he wills the overflowing happiness of his creatures.

It is no accident that precisely in the Old Testament prophecies of the future there is increasing talk of the creator and of creation. The topic is nowhere so frequent as in Deutero-Isaiah. In the redeemed humanity that is caught up in God's salvation, God's creation, which beforehand was held in check by the humans themselves, can for the first time realize itself and its own plenitude.

That can be expressed in apparently contradictory images which, however, really mean the same thing. From Mount Zion issues a stream that waters the desert and makes it fruitful (Ezekiel 47). When the glory of God shines over Zion, the pilgrimage of the nations begins, and the riches of all nations stream toward Jerusalem (Isaiah 60).

Both visions are taken up in the New Testament, where they are not dissolved, but confirmed. They form, in a sense, the frame of the whole New Testament. When the Magi from the East bring their treasures in Matt 2:11, the fulfillment of the prophetic vision of the pilgrimage of the nations is being asserted. The same is true of Rev 21:23-26, and here follows immediately the image of the river of life which flows from the throne of the Lamb (Rev 22:1-2).

God's Interest in the World Unleashes a Drama

In the theology of the twentieth century, the expression "salvation history" has often played a major role. But do we live as if there were such a thing as salvation history? Has it really penetrated the praxis and spirituality of Christians? If it has, then they must interpret the events that make up their lives, week by week and year by year, in their communities and parishes as parts of a dramatic historical action of God in a world that in part clings to him, but in part, just as decidedly, defends itself against him. Where do they actually do that? It is just such a process of interpretation that is the essence of the Bible.

We have blocked our view of this fact by means of detours in interpretation that we often fail to recognize as such. For example, in the Lord's Prayer we pray "Thy will be done." But very few are aware that this really means: "Realize the plans you have for this world." That is, "make Your will effective in this world." We think automatically of achievements expected of us which we ask God's help in accomplishing.

Still fewer have any idea what "God's will" might be. For the most part, we think solely of the keeping of the ten commandments. That is of course not wrong; it is also part of the biblical notion of the "will of God." But first, foremost, and comprehensively "God's will" means "God's plan" for the course of world history. It is a plan we already know, for God has unveiled it for us through his prophets. It consists in this: God wills to call a people together, to transform them, and through them to transform the whole world.

This idea of the will of God as plan of God is unfolded in Deutero-Isaiah and plays a part in the New Testament, especially in the letter to the Ephesians and in John's gospel. Jesus himself understood the will of God in this way. When he divorces himself in Mark 3:33 with a positively juridical formula of separation from his natural family (the so-called "holy family") and constitutes a new "family," this new family consists of people who have decided to "do the will of God" (Mark 3:35). Surely Jesus' mother and the whole holy family were faithful in keeping the ten commandments, and even the whole Torah. But apparently they did not recognize at that time that God now, at this moment, willed to act decisively in his world through one of their family members, Jesus. Therefore they regarded him as crazy and wanted to bring him back into the protective lap of the family, which is what one did with insane and disturbed people in those days. Others saw that God was here at work, and Jesus called them into his new "family." They had understood that God's "will" was dramatic and historical.

This example of the will of God shows us how deeply accustomed we are, on the basis of our upbringing, to reinterpret the "dramatic and salvation-historical" concepts of the Bible into individual commonplace or timeless, static concepts. That relieves us of the necessity to look for the action of God in the events of our lives and the history of our own times, and to interpret certain happenings as such on the basis of our faith. Only where Christian communities recognize that they must do that, because the Bible does it all the time, will talk of a solidarity of God with the poor in our world make any sense.

For then this solidarity can no longer be misunderstood as a limitation of divine love to a particular group of people. It will then express what it should express—that God's plan for the drama of the historical transformation of the corrupt human world into God's world begins in one particular phase among the poor and nowhere else.

Whoever has not learned to live and interpret "dramatically" will misunderstand the "partisanship" of God for the poor and every sort of solidarity with the "struggle" of the poor as timeless or metaphysical. But what is at issue is God's ways through and in history, which he travels with the humanity he has created.

We are at the end of our reconstruction, organized in theses, of a biblical-theological horizon for the question of the biblical shape of God's concern for the poor. If there is such a thing, it can have nothing to do with denial of the world; but rather, it takes place for the sake of the richness of God's world in a particular phase of the drama between God and his creation that is being played out in our history.

But now we must set up a second, historical horizon. What was the attitude of the world around Israel and the New Testament communities to their poor? If we do not ask this question, we run the risk of supposing that things belong to the specific biblical message of God that in fact were a common custom at that time. In that case we might fail to obtain a clear picture of what really is special about God's concern for the poor of the world.

The Contemporary Social Horizon of the Biblical Declaration of God's Special Concern for the Poor

This review is purposely restricted to the environment of the ancient Near East, from which the Old Testament stems. For the Greco-Roman world, which had at least a shared influence on the picture in Jesus' time, many similar things could be said. There are some nuances, but they are certainly not as extensive as is often supposed on the basis of Hendrik Bolkestein's classic book (*Wohltätigkeit und Armenpflege im vorchristlichen Altertum*, Utrecht, 1939). It is not true, for example, that in the Greek and Roman world care for widows and orphans was lacking. Ingomar Weiler has demonstrated the contrary, against Bolkestein (*Saeculum* 31, 1981). But the main lines of the biblical statements were developed in the Old Testament period, so that our main concern must be with the ancient Near Eastern background.

Let us begin with a statement of the principal finding: In the social ethos of Israel's surrounding societies, one certainly finds what today would be called an option for the poor. It corresponds to their idea of the gods, who were also in a very deep sense helpers of the poor. Many biblical statements, motifs, and formulations are simply participation in the thought and feeling of the whole environment in which the Bible arose.

Allow me to unfold the subject once more in a series of theses with added explanations.

In the ancient Near East, the rich were brought up to care for the poor.

The education of the upper classes in that world is reflected for us in the wisdom literature. What we have stems primarily from Egypt. Most of the Egyptian wisdom teachings are addressed to the king, because he is in a sense the ideal object of education. But what is said of him is valid for all those who are taught in the schools. As early as the end of the third millennium, in the teaching of Meri-ka-re, we read: "Soothe those who are weeping; do not afflict the widow; deprive no man of his father's goods." In the teaching of Ani from the end of the second millennium we have:

> You may not eat a meal when another is stand-ing by unless you stretch out your arm to give food to the other as well . . . The human being is nothing. One is rich, the other is poor . . . The one who last year was rich is a vagabond this year . . . You, too, may come to a point where someone gives you crumbs.

Finally, at the end of the last millennium BCE, the demotic wisdom book of Phibis (=Papyrus Insinger) says: "The one who gives food to the poor will be welcomed by the god in eternal favor. For when food is given, the heart of the god rejoices more than the heart of the one who receives it."

Every Egyptian had to try to live in such a way that, after death, she or he could declare before the divine judge of the dead what the Egyptian *Book of the Dead* prescribes in its famous 125th chapter, and which may also be found on numerous tomb inscriptions from all periods: "I gave bread to the hungry, water to the thirsty, clothing to the naked, and a passage to those who had no ship." On the tomb of Rekh-mi-Re, a vizier of Tutmose III, we read:

> I soothed tears with consolation. I defended the widows. I placed the orphans in their fathers' inheri-tance. I gave bread to the hungry and water to the thirsty; meat, oil, and clothing to those who had none. I supported the old man by giving him my staff. I caused the old woman to cry out: "Oh, how good everything is!"

From Mesopotamia, through the fortunes of archaeology, we possess far fewer wisdom texts. But from those we have, the same picture emerges. However, let us go on to a second point that concretizes this first one.

Care for the rights of the poor was a special obligation of the king.

In fact, the governing elite had a very special responsibility for the lower fringes of society, and this was particularly true of the king as head of state.

In the Canaanite epics from Ugarit, it is regarded as a typical duty of the king of a city to go in the morning to the city gate, where the citizens used to settle their legal disputes. There "he helps the widow to obtain her rights, and speaks just judgment for the orphan" (Epic of Danel).

From the middle of the third millennium onwards, the Mesopotamian kings boasted of their remission of debts and their legal reforms. They had thereby secured that "justice was visible in the land," that "the strong did not deprive the weak of their rights, and orphan and widow received their just due"—according to the formulation of the epilogue to the Codex of Hammurabi in the second millennium. The widows and orphans were, in the whole of the ancient Near East, typical examples of those who have fallen to the lower limit of the conditions for existence. In a society in which all human life was so closely integrated in the family structure, the dissolution of the family connection through the death of the relevant persons was *the* economic and social catastrophe. By the way, things have not changed so much. According to recent statistics, 80 percent of the poor in the United States are women with their children—that is to say orphans and widows, transposed into modern societal structures. But beyond these cases, the frequent general release from debts was directed primarily to those who were so deeply in debt that they had no hope of getting out again. The alternatives were forgiveness of debts or descent into the bitter fate of the day laborer, if not outright slavery. The kings of Mesopotamia forced the creditors to relinquish their demands so that the debtor was able to escape from debt into a situation in which once again economic and social freedom could determine the conditions of life. Who is there today who could force the world's major banks to do likewise?

This Mesopotamian tradition of a periodic royal restoration of economic and social point zero had no parallel in Egypt. But there, after the great social upheaval of the first inter-dynastic period, it was likewise said that God had "made the princes to strengthen the backs of the weak." Finally, at the time of Akhenaten, there emerged the formula that the king was "a god who makes princes and builds up the poor." To fully understand the saying, one has to know that the word "build up" here represents an activity normally attributed to the creator god. The king is to be for the poor like the creator, who builds up from them, as from clay, a glorious and shining creature.

This brings us directly to our third thesis.

The basis for the lofty ethic of care for the poor was the common conviction that the gods themselves, particularly the sun god, have a special love for the poor.

The sun god, appearing under different names according to the different cultures, was everywhere regarded as the god of justice and of a successful human social order. As such, the god had a special affection for the poor.

In the Akkadian "Counsels of Wisdom" from the Kassite period we read the following warning:

> Show friendship to the weak. Do not abuse those who have fallen low . . . Do not hector them imperiously. For the god who protects a human being is angered by such a thing. It displeases the sun, who will revenge it with evil. Rather, give food to eat, and beer to drink; grant what is requested, attend to it and honor the one who asks. That will please the person's protector god. It gives joy to the sun, who will reward it with favor.

In Egypt, beginning with the period of the Ramessids, there is a profusion of witnesses. The petitioner's declaration that she or he is poor is one of the central motifs of so-called "personal piety."

Researchers even speak of a "religion of the poor." For example, in a prayer to Amun we find:

> My heart longs to see you. My heart is glad, Amun, thou protector of the poor. You are the father of the orphan, the husband of the widow. How pleasant it is to speak your name. It is like the taste of life. It is like the taste of bread to a child, like a robe for the naked, like the scent of a blossoming bough in the time of the summer heat.

Those who trust in Amun are called blessed:

> Blessed are they who already are seated in Amun's hand, who protects the silent and rescues the poor . . . It is you who hears the prayer of the one who calls to you, who rescues a man from the hand of the violent.

This brings us to the special problem of the poor in the ancient Near East: it was difficult for them to uphold their rights against the rich in the courts of justice. Therefore one cried to Amun:

> Incline your ear to the one who stands alone before the judge and who is poor, not rich. The court takes silver and gold from this one's pocket for the clerk and clothing for the servant of the court. But perhaps Amun will change himself into a vizier to acquit the poor. Perhaps the poor will yet receive justice. Oh, that the poor might yet drive the rich from the field!

In Egypt, in the later period, the conviction that the gods are always on the side of the poor, even at the judgment of the dead, was so decisive that one finds statements that it is really better to be poor and to live wretchedly in this world. That kind of notion would be scarcely imaginable in the Israel of the Old Testament. But, apart from this borderline case, it should be clear by now to what a notable extent the concern for the poor that we find in the Old Testament reflects the sympathy of the whole of the ancient Near East for the victims of human society. The next thesis seeks to expand somewhat on this point.

> *Most of the Old Testament statements on the poor belong in the ancient Near Eastern cultural context, often even in their linguistic formulation.*

If we were to proceed purely on the basis of statistics, we could probably fit the great majority of the Old Testament texts that speak of "the poor" quite easily into the ancient Near Eastern picture. Of course, we have here only one God rather than many. But that in itself is brought to bear on the question of who it is who cares for the poor. In Psalm 82 the many other gods are deprived of their divinity precisely because they have not fulfilled their obligation toward the poor of the world. In this psalm, Yahweh holds judgment on the assembled gods, and formulates as a command what the real duty of the gods should be: "Give justice to the weak and the orphan, maintain the right of the oppressed and the destitute. Rescue the weak and the needy, deliver them from the hand of their oppressor." But the gods have not done that; they have judged unjustly and allowed the transgressors to rise to the top of the world's societies. Therefore they are to be deposed, and Yahweh alone will take over their task.

Since Israel had kings only in one particular period, the statements about the obligation of the king to aid the poor in obtaining their rights are rather insignificant in number. But there are enough of them to show that they fit perfectly in the general picture for the ancient Near East. For example, there is specific praise of King Josiah of Judah in Jer 22:16: "He helped the weak and the poor to obtain justice. Is not this to know me (= Yahweh)?" The ideal image of the just king is sketched in Psalm 72, and here again his righteousness consists primarily in concern for the poor. Isa 11:3-5 tells how the expected Messiah-king will create justice for the poor.

In the national as well as in the non-national periods, however, care for the poor is in any case required of all well-to-do Israelites who have been educated in the philosophy of wisdom. This is witnessed by a whole series of texts from Proverbs and Psalms.

Especially close to the ancient Near Eastern parallels are also the legislative provisions in favor of the poor in the Pentateuch, though in many cases they go far beyond their non-Israelite counterparts. If we compare the reasoning behind the so-called social critique of the prophets, we also find a close connection with ancient Near Eastern thought on the subject of the poor. And in the prayers in the psalter, Yahweh is repeatedly praised, very much as in the contemporary personal piety of Egypt, as the savior of the poor, and those who pray the Psalms refer to themselves before God as the poor, the "anawim."

All this represents a massive commonality between Israel and its surroundings; and I have really given only a few suggestions. How has biblical exegesis handled the matter?

Most exegetes seem to be quite unaware of these facts. Or are they keeping quiet about them so as not to diminish the glory of the Bible? Parallels are sometimes cited, but in such a manner as to seem to want to show that there had been tentative beginnings of a concern for the poor outside Israel which, however, first found their full development in Israel itself. But this solution is too simple and does not correspond to the facts. A very few exegetes have tried to work out some distinctions. Thus Jacques Dupont (in *Les Béatitudes*) states that in the ancient Near East it was primarily the king who took the side of the poor, while in Israel it was the deity who did this. But that also seems to me to be inaccurate, although there are certainly individual differences on particular points.

It seems better to me to acknowledge the massive similarity in concern for the poor that existed between Israel and the surrounding societies and to interpret it as such. Please note, I do not mean that the biblical statements about God's concern for the poor will thereby be exhausted and fully interpreted. But what is special in the Bible will first become clear to us when we plainly state what there is that is not at all distinctive and yet must in a real sense be called an "option for the poor."

That forces us, however, to a conclusion that I will formulate in my final thesis.

In light of the stated similarities between the Old Testament and its environment, it would seem that much that is today referred to as "option of the Church for the poor" is not in any way specifically biblical and is therefore not specifically Christian.

The matter-of-fact way in which the ancient Near East, before there was a Bible, already demanded the same treatment of the poor as do the biblical wisdom teachers and prophets shows us that we have here an issue of simple humanity that arose as soon as a society had developed to the point at which social classes, with tension between those above and below, distinction between rich and poor, were the normal order of things. Woe to that society if at that point those on the bottom did not become the first concern of those on top!

That does not mean, of course, that the will of God is not eminently expressed in the matter. God, by taking up in the Bible what the wise among the nations knew even before the Bible, confirmed it and placed himself in support of it anew. But, on the other hand, it evidently represents nothing thus far that would have remained outside human knowledge but for the revelation in the Old and New Testaments. In the early modern period, the concept of natural law was worked out, in dependence on similar concepts in ancient and medieval thought, to cover knowledge of that sort. But the concept and its philosophical definition are not the matter at issue. It is far more important to see that precisely this finding of biblical and non-biblical commonality gives Christians legitimate ground for working with all people of good will in their struggle for the rights of the poor in our world. This is, in fact, one of the concerns of Latin-American liberation theology. In the texts we have examined it can find a genuine biblical legitimation.

Certainly, in doing so we will at the same time find ourselves drawing a limit. Perhaps the theology of liberation must sometimes be more careful about saying that its demand for a common struggle, together with all people of good will, for the cause of the poor represents the essence of Christianity in itself. It could be that thereby the truly central point of the Bible has not yet been reached, and that this latter will only be visible when everything we have just been discussing is first recognized and acknowledged. There could be an option for the poor that we dare not refuse and that still does not at all represent the liberation of which the Bible speaks when it ceases to sing the same tune as the whole of the ancient Near East; when it finally raises its voice in its own melodic line to which all this other only provides the ground bass or the rhythmic accompaniment.

The questions thus raised will occupy us in the next two chapters. It may turn out that many of the biblical texts that at first sounded like echoes of the general Near Eastern option for the poor will find still another value in a specific biblical context that remains to be discovered. But in order to be able to determine whether that is so, we need first of all to set up the nonspecific material as a horizon for further investigation.

This may not be a satisfying conclusion to our initial reflections. In the next chapter, we can proceed to ask whether there is a specifically biblical concern and inclination of God for the poor that cannot be verified elsewhere in the ancient Near East; and if so, what its characteristics may be.

⤳⤳ 2 ⤳⤳

The Exodus Story
God on the Side of the Poor

Our question in this volume is: What actually happens, according to the Bible, when God takes pity on the poor? In the last chapter, we tried to set up the horizon before which the question can legitimately be asked. First, the theological horizon, for God's interest in itself is directed at something quite other than poverty. God intends plenitude and riches in his creation. God has a special love for the poor, but it should not be thought of as static and metaphysic; rather, it is only one particular act in the drama that plays itself out between God and his creation. In this drama, God's real interest is to lead the creation into wealth and plenty. Secondly, we considered the historical horizon. We saw that there was also a genuine concern for the poor in the societies surrounding Israel. In one primary sense, the Bible simply participates in it. Perhaps, as we said, a good deal that today is designated by the phrase "option for the poor" is to be located here, at the level of a common human ethic, rather than among those things one must call specifically biblical and therefore specifically Christian. That is in no way a devaluation and reduces its urgency not one iota. But it compels us to ask once more whether there is, beyond this, a specifically biblical concern and partiality of God for the poor.

Let us begin again with Israel's social environment. The concern for the poor we found there, although it compares very favorably with the ethic that shapes our modern and especially our Western society, had certain limitations. These can give us a clue to the direction in which we ought to direct our search. After that, an investigation of the Exodus and its implications will introduce us to the specifically biblical issues. By way of coda, a third brief section

23

will raise the historical question of Israel's origins and the problem of poverty in that context.

The Limits of the Ancient Near Eastern Option for the Poor

One initial limitation must be mentioned—the everywhere ob - vious *dissonance between theory and practice.* The texts often sound wonderful and heartwarming. They certainly arose out of a deep human impulse of sympathy. But the social reality often seems to have been quite different, at times really gruesome. In reading essays and books on the ancient Near East, I am continually impressed with the emphasis laid on this fact by knowledgeable authors. Thus the Egyptologist Helmut Brunner once wrote, "that Egyptian reality was far from approaching these ideals—this is the unambiguous lesson of the routine documents especially from the Ramesside and later periods" (LÄ 1, 448). The Assyriologist Jean Bottéro writes of the famous reform of the Babylonian king Ammi-saduqa: "It ameliorated the inconveniences that had occurred but failed to reform the insti- tutions that caused them" (*JESHO* 4, 161).

This remark of Bottéro's brings us to the second and more decisive limitation. The fact that practice falls short of theory is not only true of the ancient Near East and does not in itself say anything negative about the theory. The second limitation is, therefore, that it was only in extreme borderline cases that the social *systems*, whose very structure seemingly implied the existence of poor and rich, were called into question. The gods who cared for the poor, especially the sun god, were the same gods who guaranteed the eternal survival of the social structures. These structures were regarded as belonging to the order of creation, given by the gods and reflecting on earth the order of the heavenly world. The gods protected them.

This is also clear from a number of typical features of the texts under discussion. Most of them, apart from the prayers from the sphere of personal piety in the late Egyptian period, are framed from the perspective of the dominant class and of the rich. (Parenthetically: the expression "option for the poor" also comes from such a perspective.) A breath of "charitable" condescension wafts through many ancient Near Eastern texts. The key figure in care for the poor is almost always the king, the key symbol for the existing social order.

The ultimate effect of this ethic is merely to level the extremes and to avoid unbearable hardships. It thus serves to prevent sudden explosions within society, revolutions that would upset the whole complex, and in this sense it actually helps to maintain the systems that produce poverty. It is probably no accident that in Egypt the already existing ethic of care for the poor only developed its full character after the first interdynastic period. It was during that time Egypt had its first experience of slave revolts and of the anger of the lower classes that challenged the status quo.

Here we can spot the third limitation of this ethic. It even strengthens the order that produces poverty. It has, as we say, a "system stabilizing" effect, and this—here is the fourth point—in such a way that in the last instance it serves to obscure the real problem.

For this recommended way of caring for the poor, which does not disturb the system, is grounded in the divine world itself. The sun god plays the game—this game with its evil consequences—when he too regards his task as one of charitable pity. The ill effects appear especially at the point where, finally, each person presents him or herself as "poor" when praying to God and takes possession of the prayers of lament that were originally meant for those in real misery. For when all can call themselves "poor" before God, the suffering of those who are truly poor is trivialized. When everyone without exception can have exactly the same relationship to the deity as that which exists on earth between poor and rich, then poverty on earth begins to appear as a natural and necessary aspect of creation. And that is simply a lie. There is no such thing as poverty on earth out of natural necessity.

So much for the limitations of the Near Eastern option for the poor. I want to add two remarks to prevent any misunderstanding.

The first is that in some borderline instances the ancient Near Eastern society itself became aware of the limitations of its concern for the poor. When the idea emerged in Egypt, at least toward the end, that it might be better to have been poor on earth than to have been rich, and when this thought could even embed itself in the apparently popular Setna novella, then in effect the value of the this-worldly order, which is so highly praised and regarded as divinely sanctioned, is being called into question. When, in Mesopotamia, hymns were sung especially to certain goddesses, such as Ishtar, for making the poor rich and the rich poor, that is perhaps not merely praise of divine omnipotence but at the same time an expression of the suspicion that a society in which some people are poor and others rich and no one can do anything about it may not be, after all, completely in accord with the divine will. Wolfgang Röllig thinks that one could also mention in this connection the so-called rituals of an "inverted world"—such as the custom at the Babylonian Akitu festival of stripping the king for a short time of all his royal insignia, treating him like a private person and humiliating him; or the ritual of the "substitute king" carried out in times of emergency; or the suspension of all class distinctions during the feast days of a temple dedication, which Gudea mentions in one inscription from Lagash (W. Rollig in: G. Kehrer, ed., *Vor Gott sind alle gleich* [1983], 45-52). But it is not at all certain, on the one hand, that this is a correct interpretation of these texts and rites; and, on the other hand, even such a treatment allows the matter to appear only on the fringes of the ancient Near Eastern world, while the texts mandating care for the poor that were our starting point in chapter 1 are omnipresent and of central significance.

My second remark concerns the present-day option of the churches for the poor and the theology of liberation that is connected with it. I suggested in the previous chapter that these might belong more in the realm of the ancient Near Eastern option for the poor than in a specifically biblical ethic. The analysis we have just made of the limitations of the ancient Near Eastern ethic of poverty compels us to refine that suggestion. Theology of liberation is by no means directed merely to charitable assistance to the poor while preserving the structures that produce poverty. Rather, it sees clearly that the social structures are themselves "sinful" and wants to change them. In this respect, it goes far beyond the ancient Near East. At most, one can question whether it is following the specifically biblical route to change; or whether, in its description of the methods for social transformation, it has not stopped halfway.

But this question can really be proposed only after we have grasped the distinctively biblical approach by means of an analysis of the theology of the Exodus. That is our next step.

The Exodus
Prototype of God's Concern for the Poor

The Exodus, the deliverance of Israel from Egypt at the beginning of its history by its God, Yahweh, is the central, in fact the unique, theme of the Old Testament confession of faith. In this event, Yahweh carried out a fundamental, constitutive act in and for his people. And this action was a divine act of liberation on behalf of poor and oppressed people.

Before we turn to the individual texts, a word of clarification about method. I am not interested, at the moment, in using a historical method to reconstruct the events behind the biblical version of the Exodus. I intend, of course, to say something about Israel's historical origins; but that will come later, both in time and in order of importance, in some sense only as a coloring in of a picture whose contours are already sharply drawn. If I may borrow Brevard Childs's terminology, my purpose throughout is to depict the "canonical" shape of the Exodus theology. I am concerned with what the definitive Bible, the Word of God as we have it in our hands, tells us about the Exodus. For that, one need not, for example, to do a tradition-critical analysis of the Exodus theme; and one certainly need not restrict oneself to the oldest texts and witnesses. Rather, it is a question of the statements about Israel's deliverance from Egypt that Jesus and his disciples could also read in their sacred Scriptures. I am interested in the Old Testament Exodus theology in all its richness and in all its variety, but also in its full depth. From the point of view of literary criticism, this depth may first have been reached after centuries of human thought and meditation; and many more of Israel's experiences in later centuries may have contributed to the final formulation of the Exodus theme. But all of this together resulted in the Word of God about Yahweh's concern for the poor, condensed in the prototypical event of the Exodus.

The classic formulation of the Exodus credo is in Deut 26:5-10. It is the confession of faith that the Israelite father spoke when, accompanied by his entire family, he brought the first fruits of the harvest to the sanctuary.

The great Old Testament master of my own student days, Gerhard von Rad, as most of you may already know, built a whole theory of the origins of the Pentateuch on this text. He believed it to be an ancient prayer from the early period of the Judges, and as such in a sense the form-critical seed of the whole Hexateuch, which was nothing but a long narrative expansion of this little confession of faith to positively baroque proportions. Von Rad's theory has proved untenable. This credo is not so early. It was shaped by a deuteronomist hand and presumes at least the older sources of the Pentateuch (Yahwist and Elohist, according to classical Pentateuch theory). It is certainly a wonderful text, in any case, summarizing, as it does, these old sources for the use of the new divine worship in the central sanctuary of the deuteronomic reform.

The pattern which the deuteronomist author used for his new credo was to be found in the ancient documents themselves, and we still have it. According to Num 20:14-21, Moses sent messengers to the king of Edom to obtain his permission to pass through his land. The message he gave them contains a kind of very brief summary of the history of Israel. It reads:

Our fathers went down to Egypt, and we dwelt in Egypt a long time; and the Egyptians dealt harshly with us, as with our fathers.

Then we cried to Yahweh, and he heard our cry. He sent an angel who brought us forth out of Egypt. (Num 20:15-16)

This is, in fact, the oldest historical summary that we have from Israel. It also presupposes and summarizes the old Pentateuchal sources. Poverty and rescue from it are not its special themes, though the topics of poverty and the oppression of Israel in Egypt were already present in manifold form in the old sources. It is a summary shaped entirely with an eye to a family or national history, so that monetary relationships are rather discreetly omitted. It is therefore all the more surprising that the credo in Deuteronomy 26, which is modelled on this first historical resume, makes the themes of "pov - erty" and "deliverance from poverty" its central ideas. Let us now take a look at this credo from Deuteronomy. It reads:

> A wandering Aramean was my father; and he went down to Egypt and sojourned there, few in number; and there he became a nation, great, mighty, and populous.
>
> The Egyptians treated us harshly, impoverished us and laid upon us hard bondage.
>
> Then we cried to Yahweh, the God of our fathers, and Yahweh heard our cry and saw our poverty, our toil, and our affliction.
>
> And Yahweh brought us out of Egypt with a mighty hand and an outstretched arm, with great terror, with signs and wonders; and he brought us into this place and gave us this land, a land flowing with milk and honey.
>
> And behold, now I bring the first of the fruit of the ground, which thou hast given me, O Yahweh! (Deut 26:5-10)

This central Old Testament text alone should silence anyone who finds it embarrassing for Christian churches to speak of an "option for the poor" and for a theology to call itself "liberation theology." This credo is above all a confession of the God who led the poor into freedom. If the credo of the New Testament adds new dimensions, it certainly never falls short of this credo of Israel.

This credo, as I have said, refers back in its themes of "poverty," "affliction," and "liberation," and even in its vocabulary to material that is to be found in the extended stories in the older levels of Pentateuchal material in the book of Exodus. The later priestly Pentateuch source will lay even more emphasis on these aspects of the text of Exodus, especially that of oppression. Many other texts spread throughout the Old Testament echo these. Even, and espe- cially, Israel's laws, where they speak of the poor and the stranger, repeatedly recall the situation in Israel at the beginning of its history as a people, when it was in Egypt. Think, for example, of Exod 23:9:

> You shall not exploit a stranger; you know the heart of a stranger, for you were strangers in the land of Egypt.

We thus have in the credo of Deuteronomy 26 the quintessence of Israel's faith, and it is neither accident nor exaggeration that it is entirely subsumed under the theme of liberation. We have a perfect right to proceed on the basis of this very text to inquire about what is specifically biblical; to seek to discover what distinguishes the concern of Yahweh, the God of Israel, for the poor from the care of the other gods of the ancient Near East for their poor.

Oddly enough, the basic outlines of the credo reveal at first a close parallelism with the theology of poverty in the whole of the ancient Near East. We see that the primary text of the credo has the following scheme of action (which, incidentally, was already concealed in the basic story of the book of Exodus as a whole):

1. People are in distress.

2. They cry out to a god.

3. The god hears their cry and sees their distress.

4. The god intervenes and alleviates the distress.

We could call this an anthropological proto-scheme or proto-model. It was constantly presented to the minds of people in ancient cultures through the inner structure of lament and thanksgiving liturgies and in the prayers they used. We find it repeatedly in the laments and songs of thanksgiving in the psalter. Israel knew it as well as did the surrounding cultures.

It has been shown that many of the texts concerning the poor in the ancient Near East had their spiritual home in this context of lament and thanksgiving. So Israel took up precisely this point when it said of its God Yahweh that he is a God who has led the poor into freedom. Where else could it begin? It began with the language it had learned to speak within its own environment. But what will happen to this common language in light of God's new action in Israel's history? It is crucial to discover this, and that is our concern at the moment. I will try to proceed step by step from the common to the particular.

Just as in the lament and thanksgiving liturgies, in the texts from the ancient Near East, the god's sympathetic aid was always directed to individual poor people or to small groups from the lower classes of the population who were in particular distress. We also find, of course, the lament and the thanksgiving of a whole nation in cases of national distress. But then the nation is like a single person. In the case of the Exodus, on the other hand, we have something just halfway between these two possibilities. The focus is on a very large and inclusive group within the population of a whole country, which is recognized as a group of poor and oppressed people and then is rescued. Deuteronomy formulates this at one point in astonished tones:

> Or has any god ever attempted to go to a nation and take
> it for himself from the midst of another nation, by trials, by
> signs, by wonders, and by war, by a mighty hand and an
> outstretched arm, and by great terrors, according to all that
> Yahweh, your God, did for you in Egypt before your eyes?
> (Deut 4:34)

From the formulae, we can clearly see that this is a kind of commentary on the credo of Deuteronomy 26. Apparently the taking of "a nation from the midst of another nation" is regarded as something thoroughly unusual. I surmise that we must understand this as referring to the whole exploited lower class of Egypt. That is, we have to ask ourselves how the Hebrews appear in the literary representation in the book of Exodus, without taking account of our historical knowledge of the facts. If we look closely, we see that they seem to be the only exploited people in Egypt. They are simply the Egyptian lower class. No other lower class people appear. The exceptions prove the rule: In two verses, at Exod 12:38 and Num 11:4, there is talk of a non-Israelite "rabble" from Egypt. But in both places, we read that this rabble also left Egypt along with the Israelites. We have to read the story in the first chapter of Exodus, according to which the Pharaoh did not remember Joseph and decided to put the Hebrews to slave labor, to oppress them, and to decimate their offspring, not only as an historical statement, but also as a kind of exemplary narrative. It portrays the way in which tension between upper and lower orders comes about in a human society—out of fear on the part of the few on top of the vital strength of the many below, whom they learn to regard as foreign to their own group. Therefore, the Hebrews, whom Yahweh leads out of Egypt through Moses, are not some group among many other groups from the Egyptian underclass who may be singled out because of their family ancestry; instead, they represent the underclass as such in every major society. Concretely, this particular one bears the name of Egypt.

But whether one accepts this interpretation of the group called "Israel" in the context of the Exodus testimony or not, the poor are here in any case a large group within a larger society, and thus exceed the dimensions that are normally envisioned in connection with lament and thanksgiving. Now for a second step.

The misery of these poor is clearly explained in the credo of Deuteronomy 26 as resulting from economic exploitation and social degradation. The system-related nature of poverty, the fact that it is produced by human wickedness—these are named for what they are. This is also given explicit narrative expression in chapter one of the book of Exodus. There the king of Egypt decrees the oppression. Later, in the fifth chapter, when Moses and Aaron try to negotiate with him, he intensifies the oppression through a new, deliberate decision. Poverty is thus clearly recognized here as the product of human action. It is neither fate, nor the will of the gods, nor deserved because of personal fault. The symbolic figure of the social system, the Pharaoh, has willed it and effected it.

But now we come to the decisive third step of our analysis. Yahweh's intervention does not aim, as do such acts of assistance elsewhere in the ancient Near East, to lighten the suffering while leaving the system intact or perhaps even aiding its renewed stabilization. Instead, the poor are removed from the impoverishing situation. Nowhere else in the ancient Near East have I encountered in the context of divine aid to the poor even the remotest suggestion that a god might physically remove the poor who cry to him or her from the world that oppresses them as human beings.

We are so accustomed to hearing the Exodus story that we scarcely sense the enormity of this idea. The astonishment that echoes in the text cited from Deut 4:34 may help to make clear to us what an audacious notion it is. In the first place, from everything the ancient Near Eastern texts tell us, we would have expected only that Yahweh would hear the cry of the poor and come to their aid in Egypt. That would correspond to what we ourselves try to do with our development aid for the needs of the Third World. If we look beyond the horizon of the ancient Near East, we might perhaps have expected that Yahweh would have tried to reform the system by means of a revolution or a peaceful negotiation between his servants and the Pharaoh. That would be, if I see the situation rightly, like what we normally have in mind today in the Third World or at home when we speak of the "option for the poor" and of "theology of liberation." But Yahweh does more; he takes the poor completely outside the Egyptian system.

When I have presented this exegesis in the past, people have often told me that it is an over-interpretation of the Bible, that I am trying to read things into it that the Bible itself does not intend in such a brutal fashion. Consequently, it seems important to me to spend some time on this point. I personally am convinced that the authors and redactors of the book of Exodus were thoroughly aware of the questions I have posed and that they have given a quite unambiguous answer to them in their own narrative fashion. In the book of Exodus they have certainly told all sorts of stories; and in the past I have often wondered why they made such a complicated narrative out of the people's being led out of Egypt. Couldn't it have been a lot simpler? But I have come to believe that it was precisely our complex of questions that guided them. I will make a brief attempt to clarify this statement.

The narrative in the book of Exodus recounts quite deliberately, it seems to me, a series of attempts to aid the exploited Hebrews in some way other than their removal from Egypt.

Immediately after the beginning of the oppression, the daughter of the Pharaoh practices the ancient Egyptian royal concern for an individual poor person, with which we are by now familiar, when she rescues the exposed child Moses from death. In fact, she goes so far as to make him her son, which is definitely no small matter (Exod 2:1-10). But the story goes on as if nothing had happened, thus leading by its very structure to the pregnant question: What good do such individual acts of charity do for the other poor people?

Moses begins his career as liberator soon afterward with counter-terror when he kills an especially brutal oppressor. But the system is too powerful. Its structures of fear have already been so interiorized by the oppressed themselves that they want nothing to do with such a terrorist. They see in him only a person who, when he has helped them, will then exercise brutality toward them in turn. That is usually what happens when the poor are aided within the system by such means. They are not really so badly mistaken. Moses has to flee from Egypt. Nothing changes there (Exod 2:11-15).

Later Moses and Aaron attempt, through negotiations with the Pharaoh, to achieve an amelioration of the condition of the oppressed people within the system. In Marxist categories one would call that a "reformist" or "revisionist" method and, according to one's particular point of view, either approve or condemn it. In the biblical narrative, this attempt at reform only makes the situation worse. The Pharaoh intensifies the burdens of the poor until they are no longer bearable (Exod 5:1-23).

Finally, the meaning of the long story of the plagues in Egypt (Exod 7:1-11:10) seems to me to be that an inhuman system eventually and necessarily brings catastrophe on itself. The fact that God himself imposes the various plagues need not distract us. Everything that happens in history has, on the one hand, a mundane cause, and, on the other hand, depends on God's disposing will. And the Bible represents things sometimes from the one perspective and sometimes from the other. This is clearly to be seen in the prophet's threats of disaster, but the same can be said of the story of the plagues. Even if the individual plagues are announced by Moses and Aaron in the name of Yahweh, it is at the same time true that this Egyptian system, which despises and exploits people, is creating for itself a self-destructive and fatal sphere of action that in the end will drag both the people and nature itself into the pit. But the catastrophes that now commence, and that follow one another with growing intensity, do not lead to insight, but instead cause the protagonists to become increasingly rigid in their evil attitudes. Therefore, we find precisely at this point the theme of the "hardening" of the Pharaoh. In such a context the presumption of "historical materialism," that it is precisely the inevitable catastrophe of an unjust system that, in a sort of natural process, serves to call forth the next stage of improved humanity, appears rather strange. The Bible is here probably closer to reality.

All these events represent, then, other ways by which one could try to put an end to a situation of oppression and impoverishment. According to the book of Exodus, they are of no use. God has another way of dealing with the situation. He leads people out of the system. That was his announced intention from the beginning, and that is what he finally does after the last and greatest "plague" and in connection with it.

The "Exodus" is something so appalling that even the victims of the system who are thereby to be set free cannot conceive or accept it, as shown by the many stories in the books of Exodus and Numbers of Israel's grumbling in the wilderness. This grumbling begins as early as Exod 14:10-12 and occasions the miracle at the Sea of Reeds. These complaints arise again and again out of homesickness for Egypt, no matter how great was the misery there.

The enormity, the immensity surpassing human imagination, of the divine solution to the problem of poverty that is summarized in the word "Exodus" leads to another, fourth step in our analysis. A deed like this is impossible for human beings. In the Exodus, the removal of the poor from the system that enslaves them is the work of Yahweh alone. Everything the Bible says about the Exodus is intended to represent it as a miracle. The formulae of the credo in Deuteronomy 26 do this through a multiplication of miracle terminology: "mighty hand and outstretched arm, great terror, signs and wonders." The narrative representation in the book of Exodus shows it by means of a story of an event that breaks all the laws of nature: the passage through the divided sea, a narrative motif that would immediately call to the mind of anyone in the ancient Near East images of the creator God who divided the monster Chaos (Exodus 14).

This brings us immediately to a further, fifth step. The creator God creates something. The product of his battle with chaotic nothingness is cosmos, a new order. The departure from the corrupt and therefore impoverishing world of Egypt would not have been a divine miracle, a new work of creation, if it had not at the same time marked the beginning of something new and greater—and this, of course, on the same level with that of the departure itself. If it marks the departure from an old society, it must be at the same time an entry into a new society.

We should not be misled by the biblical formulation into a false minimal interpretation. In the basic text in which God's appearance in the burning bush is narrated (Exod 3:8), as well as in the last sentence of the credo in Deuteronomy 26, we find the ancient expression about the "land flowing with milk and honey." As the philologist of ancient languages, H. C. Usener, demonstrated as early as 1902 in an impressive collection of materials, in the whole ancient world "milk and honey" were the Elysian food of the gods. What we have, then, is an image of the plenitude of paradise. This plenitude is, of course, only to be found where the prototypical form of life together also had its locus. The land flows with milk and honey as food for human beings there, where they live in the society intended by God from the time of creation. Only with that echo in the back of our minds can we understand why the Israelite father, bringing a basket to the sanctuary that presumably contains grain, grapes, figs, and olives, still declares emphatically that Yahweh has brought him into the land "flowing with milk and honey."

In this event the poor of Egypt can be brought into this land of Elysian happiness, according to the narrative thread of the Penta-teuch, only because on the way there they have been recreated, at the mountain of God, to form a new society. God's presence lives in the midst of this society. It arises from a festival, and that is why Yahweh

had demanded of the Pharaoh from the beginning that he let Israel
go into the desert to celebrate a feast for him. But what is meant is a
real and quite normal society. Therefore, the Bible collects all the
laws of Israel at just this point. The point of this is that the departure
from the impoverishing society was not a genuine removal unless it
led to the constitution of a new society that knows no more poverty.
Even if the Sinai tradition originally, from the point of view of
tradition criticism, had nothing to do with the Exodus tradition—incidentally, I consider this hypothesis incorrect—still, the canonical
form of the Pentateuch demands the constitution of a new society at
Sinai as an essential step between the departure from Egypt and the
entry into the land flowing with milk and honey. This alone explains
why the first led to the second.

There is a short deuteronomic version of the credo in Deut
6:20-25 which makes this connection clear:

> When your son asks you in time to come: "Why do you
> keep the testimonies and the statutes and the ordinances which
> Yahweh, our God, has commanded you?"
>
> Then you shall say to your son: "We were Pharaoh's
> slaves in Egypt; and it was Yahweh who brought us out of
> Egypt with a mighty hand; and Yahweh showed signs and
> wonders, great and grievous, against Egypt and against Phar-
> aoh and all his household, before our eyes; and he brought us
> out from there, that he might bring us in and give us the land
> which he swore to give to our fathers.
>
> And Yahweh commanded us to do all these statutes, to
> fear Yahweh our God, for our good as long as we live, and he
> will give us life, as at this day.
>
> And justice will rule among us, as long as we keep this
> whole social order before Yahweh our God and put it into
> action as he has commanded us."

In the context of the book of Deuteronomy, of course, the
primary reference is to the social order proposed in the laws of
Deuteronomy itself. According to this order, Yahweh intends that
Israel be a nation of sisters and brothers in which there will be no
more poor (cf. Deut 15:4). This in itself makes clear that, according

to the Bible, the poor of Egypt are to become, through the Exodus, a kind of divinely-willed contrast-society.

The elucidation of the concept of "contrast-society" is the sixth and last step in our analysis of the theology of the Exodus. It follows necessarily from what has gone before. In fact, the new society that Yahweh creates out of the poor Hebrews through the Exodus is not only in contrast to the Egyptian society they have left behind, but beyond that it is in contrast to all other existing societies in their world. Deuteronomy makes this explicit by saying that this new society finally embodies what all human societies long and strive for, but never really attain—"culture," which was expressed at that time in words that we normally translate as "wisdom" and "education."

This task of the society that Yahweh brings into being when he acts in and for the poor in Egypt, a task directed, however, to the good of all humanity, is perhaps most clearly expressed, among the Pentateuchal texts structured on the basis of Exodus theology, in a passage from Deuteronomy 4:

> You shall keep them and do them [i.e., these statutes and ordinances]; for that will be your wisdom and your understanding, which the nations seek.
>
> When anyone reads these laws to them, they will cry: "Surely this great nation is a wise and understanding people!"
>
> For what great nation is there that has gods so near to it as Yahweh our God was to us, whenever we have called on him [for help]?
>
> And what great nation is there, that has statutes and ordinances so righteous as all this social order which I set before you this day? (Deut 4:6-8)

This "otherness" of Israel can also be expressed in quite different, namely in sacral categories. In that case, God's new society is placed in much the same relationship to the other nations as, within an ancient society, the people who belonged to the sacred sector were related to those in the profane sector. This is the image in the text which, at a relatively late date, was placed before the whole Sinai pericope as a kind of key to it:

> You have seen what I did to the Egyptians, and how I
> bore you on eagles' wings and brought you to myself.
>
> Now, therefore, if you will listen to my voice and keep
> the vow you have sworn to me, you shall be my own possession
> among all peoples; for all the earth is mine, but you shall be
> to me a kingdom of priests and a holy nation. (Exod 19:4-6)

This, then, is God's care for the poor as it meets us in the Exodus
credo. Since this credo is linked to the beginning of Israel's history,
we ought to touch at least briefly on the question to what degree we
not only find here something like a summary of the whole Old
Testament revelation, which is undoubtedly the case; but also in what
sense the historical beginnings of Israel are correctly understood and
described in this credo. If that is the case, then the further question
arises: To what extent was Israel's beginning as a contrast-society
maintained and developed in its later history. These are, as I indicated
at the beginning of this section, not the central questions for a
"canonical" reading of the Old Testament. But, as people with
modern historical consciousness, we should not push them fully
aside. Therefore, in a third and very brief section of this chapter, I
will add several remarks on these questions.

The Exodus Theology and Israel's Historical Beginnings

The picture of a great military conquest of the land of Canaan
by a nomadic Israel that already existed as a nation of twelve tribes,
as perhaps most recently defended with bravura by W.F. Albright, is
today supported in this form by few scholars. But the counter-theory
as well, of a gradual and peaceful settlement by small groups of sheep-
and goat-herders, represented in Europe primarily by Albrecht Alt
and Martin Noth, is also being abandoned. The picture appears more
and more complicated. One must probably distinguish a variety of
groups: immigrants from distant regions, as far away as Mesopotamia, who were seeking a new homeland; border nomads in the
process of settling down; socially homeless groups of Hapiru; rural
people from the land of Canaan itself who withdrew from the areas
controlled by the Canaanite city-states and resettled in the freedom

of the hill country. One of these various groups was probably the one which had experienced the Exodus from Egypt and could tell of this great deed of its God, Yahweh.

There must then at some time have come a point at which the whole complex of groups which had gathered into the tribal farming society of "Israel" perceived the previous history of the group that had come out of Egypt as their own and narrated it as the beginning of Israel as a whole. This can only be explained if all these people had had analogous experiences in the events of their past history, which this story of the Exodus from Egypt expressed better than any other.

Evidently all these groups of people were victims of their respective societies: oppressed, poor, exploited, social and economic losers of one sort or another. Why does anyone leave the homeland and seek a new one in some distant place? Why do farmers break up their homes in the fertile valley under cover of darkness and begin a new life in the rough hills? Why does someone become a Hapiru, a person who has no place in the established order and makes a living as a robber or mercenary? Why is anyone a wandering shepherd instead of having a settled home? In details, the situation may have been very different, but they could all recognize themselves in the poor Hebrews from Egypt.

All of them had at some time, in one way or another, broken the ties to their old society, some of them willingly, others unwillingly; some gradually, others suddenly; some with a goal in mind, others simply plunging into emptiness and the unknown. But they could all understand what it means to take leave of a society.

And what now bound them together as the new entity called "Israel" was precisely the ideal of a new life together. The rural egalitarian and segmented tribal society, "Israel," was in its own self-understanding a contrast to the feudal Canaanite city-states in the vicinity as well as to their colonial overlords from far-away Egypt. They needed no walled cities because their brotherly and sisterly solidarity was a better protection. They had no social classification of poor and rich because they recognized no authority over them - selves except that of their God Yahweh; and they had developed social mechanisms to insure that equality of land ownership and in decision making was repeatedly restored. Thus, on the other end of the bridge thrown out by the Exodus story, in the entry into the land flowing with milk and honey, they were able to discern quite clearly what wonders Yahweh, to their own astonishment, had done with all of them.

In this sense, the Exodus narrative, although supposedly only the tradition of the experiences of one small group in later Israel, was nevertheless also a true story of the beginnings of all Israel.

Israel was from the very beginning a contrast-society founded in the Exodus of the poor. This society had a long and restless history, a history filled not only with high points, but even more with catastrophes. The image proposed in the beginning, at the Exodus, was repeatedly betrayed. So it came about that there were poor people in Israel, again and again. The question of poverty had to be spelled out over and over from the beginning, and it often happened that they were in exactly the same position as all the other ancient Near Eastern societies. That is why the social criticism of the prophets, the sayings of the wisdom teachers in the schools, the prayers we find in the Psalter often show such great similarity to the statements on poverty in the rest of the ancient Near East. On the basis of the Exodus theme, that should never have been the case. That is why the demand behind the statements on care for the poor in Israel is so different, despite all the similarity of the statements themselves to those made in other societies. For the demand made explicit in the Exodus credo was still valid; and an Israel that had poor people in its midst and, therefore, had to formulate an ethic of concern for the poor could really only be red-faced with shame. It was simply unacceptable that there should be poor people in Israel (see Deut 15:4).

In considering the exact meaning of the words "gospel for the poor" in the next chapter, we will have to take up this discrepancy between Israel's beginning as reflected in its credo and its often so sorry reality. But now, in conclusion, let me cast a final glance at the theology of liberation and its relationship to the Exodus statement.

There are very few complexes of biblical testimony to which the theologians of liberation refer so often as that concerning the Exodus from Egypt. In this, they doubtless betray a precise sense of what in the Bible is not only important, but decisive.

Nevertheless, I have the feeling that, at least in my church, neither the theologians of liberation nor their critics have grasped the Exodus statement in the fullness of its surprising otherness, an otherness which remains astonishing for us as well.

Liberation theologians see the Exodus as a message of political liberation, which is to be followed by other dimensions of liberation, including the human and religious. Moses appears in their work as the prototype of the "Christian politician" involved in power strug - gles, party politics, and concrete compromises. Jesus and his disciples then follow later as prototypes of ecclesial-pastoral proclamation of the gospel.

On the other side, for example, the Roman "International Theological Commission" in its 1976 document which took a critical but essentially favorable attitude to liberation theologians, empha- sized that the deliverance from Egypt was not directed to release from poverty but to the worship of God at Mount Sinai. This latter is certainly correct, but what is the context of this worship service? It is the beginning of God's new society in this world—the society in contrast to all previous societies, the contrast-society of the people of God!

The central role which the creation of a people of God plays in the Exodus seems to be as foreign to the thought of many liberation theologians as to that of the theological commission. One has the impression that, although they talk a lot about the Exodus, they do not really reckon, in the last analysis, with a genuine *departure or emigration* of the poor and with the emergence of a new society of emigres. Their Moses does not, in a sense, stop negotiating with the Pharaoh; and one day he may well even become Minister of Culture, or some other high official in the Pharaoh's court, as did the Egyptian Joseph who, according to the Bible, in fact saved the lives of the Egyptian farmers; but in the process deprived them of their cattle and land and made them subjects of a national revenue system (cf. Gen 47:13-26).

It seems to me, at least, that the liberation theologians' interpretation of the Exodus often sounds that way. In the meantime, however, the reality of the growing basic communities, not even envisioned in the original contributions to a theology of liberation, has intervened. At least some of them escape any definition as mere groups for social action or as "purely religious" gatherings for preaching and celebration of the Eucharist. They are in themselves precisely what was envisioned as the goal of the Exodus credo in ancient Israel—places for social transformation. In them, it is often really the case that the poor from country and barrio are assembled for a new life in contrast to all that went before, a life built on the memory of Israel and of Jesus.

The liberation theologians have perceived this miracle with astonishment and have begun to speak of a "Church of the poor." Could they not learn from the biblical portrayal of the Exodus, if they would take another look at it, a new way of formulating the specific aim and object of God's "option for the poor," his liberating action among and for the poor; that is, a new society which is emerging as Church from among the liberated poor? It is first of all from this Church that the transformation and salvation of the entire society can dialectically proceed. But more on this in the next chapter.

~~≈≼ 3 ≽≈~~

God and the Poor in the Bible

When Jesus of Nazareth began his public life he proclaimed good news. In two key texts in the synoptic gospels, this message is called a "gospel for the poor."

John the Baptizer, in prison, sends two disciples to Jesus to ask him: "Are you he who is to come?" Jesus answers: "the blind receive their sight and the lame walk, lepers are cleansed and the deaf hear, and the dead are raised up, and the poor have good news preached to them." The saying about the gospel (=good news) for the poor is certainly not, in this context, the last of a series of statements. It is the high point of the statement, and also a summary of the whole (Matt 11:4-6; Luke 7:22-23).

Luke begins his account of Jesus' public life with the scene in the synagogue at Nazareth. There Jesus reads aloud from the book of Isaiah:

> The Spirit of the Lord is upon me, because he has anointed me to preach good news to the poor. He has sent me to proclaim release to the captives and recovering of sight to the blind, to set at liberty those who are oppressed, to proclaim the acceptable year of the Lord.

Jesus comments on the text by saying, "Today this scripture has been fulfilled in your hearing." The key concept in this passage is undoubtedly the "good news to the poor." It is only spelled out in the clauses that follow (Luke 4:18-21).

Talk of the "gospel for the poor" plays a major role in the theology of liberation. Jon Sobrino, one of the most important liberation theologians of the second generation, perhaps the one with the greatest gift for systematic theology, once wrote: "The gospel of Jesus is a gospel for the poor. Only someone who is poor can understand this gospel at all."

Is that true? Only a person who is hungry can really understand what it means when someone says: "Soup's on!" I think that in this sense Sobrino's statement is quite correct. Nevertheless, I think that we ought to investigate somewhat more closely to discover who are the poor to whom Jesus' gospel is directed. That is the task I have chosen for this third chapter.

Before I begin, allow me once more to recall that I have no intention of trying to exhaust the subject of God and the poor in the Bible. That would be impossible in one small volume. My intention is only to select some questions that, in the context of the present-day option of the churches for the poor, are perhaps especially in need of a biblical perspective. Therefore, we began this volume with a look at the question of the horizons, both theological and historical, of all the biblical statements on the poor and poverty. Theologically, we saw that God does not intend poverty and misery for his creation, but rather wealth and plenty; and that God's special concern for the poor thus can never be understood in a static-metaphysical sense, but only as a phase in the historical drama between God and humanity. Historically, we found that there was already, before the Bible, a notable ethos of care for the poor in which the Bible participates to a considerable extent. On that basis, we posed the question whether the churches' concern for the poor, however much it corresponds to God's will in the matter, can be regarded as distinctively biblical and Christian. We last took up this question of what is really distinctive in the Bible. I presented an interpretation of the Old Testament credo of the Exodus—a thematic complex which is also basic for much of liberation theology. We saw that in this instance poor people are not just given some kind of aid; instead, the social system that produced their poverty is rejected in toto. They are removed from this system, and God creates out of them the miracle of a new society in contrast to all previous societies, a society in which there are no more poor. The beginning of a divine contrast-society—that is God's concrete and distinctive option for the poor in the meaning of the Exodus credo. Has the theology of liberation really recognized this? It knows—and that is already a great deal—that the very structures of our society must be challenged. Does it also know how God challenges them? That he does so by creating a people of God as contrast-society, and by no other means?

Clearly, this is far from the whole of what could be said, on the basis of the Old Testament, about God's concern and care for the poor. In the same sense, our subject here is a selection from the many statements in the New Testament. But this topic has a special uniqueness. On the one hand, it will of itself lead us back once again from the New Testament to the Old. But on the other hand, it is in a certain sense the central theme when one seeks an answer to the question of God and the poor in the New Testament.

With the Baptizer's question, at any rate, we have already touched the motherlode of the gospel tradition. The subject of "the poor" and "poverty" is in fact dominant in the oldest traditional materials of the Gospels. In the later strata of the Gospels, on the contrary, and especially in the other parts of the New Testament, it recedes in importance. It is nowhere fully absent, and if we come to the New Testament from the Old, we soon discover that it is much more broadly represented than a search for the word "poverty" and its cognates would at first indicate. For one recognizes, on that basis, that sickness and every sort of marginalizing are parts of the same subject. So is persecution, and whoever has eyes to see will soon suspect, and rightly so, that even Paul's theology of the cross is connected with it.

Nonetheless, the decline in the occurrence of the words for "poor" that were so common in the Old Testament is striking. And we get very little information from the early Christian communities, whose life is clearly reflected in the New Testament, about poor people and aid for the poor. For example, how seldom do those sections of the letters in the New Testament that give advice on community life say anything on this subject! But if one thinks about the Exodus theology, this is really not so remarkable. For, according to that theology, it is God's intention that there be a society in which there are no more poor. And if God has already sent his Messiah, where should we look for that society if not in the New Testament

communities? In the New Testament exegetical literature, I have
found every possible explanation of the rare occurrence of the theme
of "poverty," including the suggestion that the early Christians were
so occupied with their internal community concerns that they had no
time for contemporary social problems. But I have very seldom
encountered the notion that among the early Christians, because of
a new initiative in common life given them by Jesus and a new way
of handling material goods, there might have been something like an
abolition of social stratification and the disappearance of real pov -
erty. The sentence in the Acts of the Apostles that explicitly says this
about the original community—"There was not a needy person
among them" (Acts 4:34)—is usually suspected of being ideological
in nature and dismissed as "idealistic portrayal" or as an importation
of Greek "philosophical utopianism." The theologians of liberation
cite it, but it does not really play a central role in their thinking. I
would like, on the contrary, at least to pose the question whether the
New Testament, apart from its oldest levels, does not perhaps have
so little to say about the poor because in the early communities, the
world had really changed.

In any case, this situation in the later New Testament corpus
makes it all the more important that, in the very oldest traditions
contained in the Gospels, the theme of poverty is still central. For
there we can get in touch with the beginning of it all. What exactly
do we find there?

We cannot correctly understand the saying about a "gospel" for
the poor unless we recognize it as an allusion to Old Testament texts
that would have echoed in the minds of Jesus and his contemporaries
when the key word was mentioned. The formulation itself—"to bring
good news to the poor"—does not originate with Jesus, but comes
from Isa 61:1. Jesus uses it in his reply to John's disciples in a citation
made up of texts from Isa 29:18-19; 35:5-6; 42:18; and 61:1. The
logic of his answer to John is: You are waiting for the one of whom
Isaiah speaks; well, are Isaiah's words being fulfilled? The reference
to Isaiah was supposed to be recognized as such, and no doubt it was.
In the scene in the synagogue at Nazareth, we have a corresponding
situation. Jesus reads the text of Isa 61:1-2 from the roll as a scriptural
message—even if Luke has abridged it and then expanded it with

elements from Isa 58:6. Here it is also clear that when Jesus proclaims good news for the poor, it is not something new, but only the definitive and eschatologically effective proclamation of the arrival, now beginning, of this thing that has long existed as promise.

The catchword "gospel for the poor," then, means a gospel that was proclaimed in Israel at least since the book of Isaiah was written. To find out what it means, who are the poor in this context, and what are the joyful tidings that are to be spoken to them, we have to consult Isaiah, and in fact the whole of the Old Testament. The most important portion of text is Isaiah 40-55, the so-called book of Deutero-Isaiah. There is the first appearance of the word "gospel" in the Bible, and at the very outset it is a gospel for Yahweh's poor. But first I would like to refer briefly to a precursor of Deutero-Isaiah from the time before the Exile, the prophet Zephaniah. Afterward, I want to touch briefly on the subsequent history of Deutero-Isaiah in the Old Testament.

Zephaniah
and the Future Israel of the Poor

I want to discuss Zephaniah specifically because one of the most influential books in recent decades on the subject of God and the poor, Albert Gelin's *Les pauvres de Yahvé* (The Poor of Yahweh), 1952, takes Zephaniah as its very starting point, and makes this prophet the father of the whole so-called Anawim-movement. He sees the concept of poverty as already totally spiritualized there—an interpretation which influenced the development of the whole book.

With Gelin, and against most of my colleagues (in Europe at least), I consider the book of Zephaniah preexilic, with the exception of a few verses inserted in the main text and, especially, those added at the end. Nothing in the main text itself presupposes the Babylonian exile, and certainly not the end of exile. The book is a synopsis of the message of Zephaniah, who emerged as a prophet in Jerusalem and Judah at the time of King Josiah of Judah and probably before Josiah's deuteronomic reform. In recent times the understanding of the book has been much obscured because it has been read and discussed only in fragmentary fashion. It seems to me that the book makes its particular statement primarily in its structure as a whole, a structure that is determined to an unusual degree by the principles of chiasm and ring-composition, to whose clarification the Berkeley Old Testament scholar, Duane Christensen, has made such an important contribution. I cannot describe all this in detail at this point; I will only give some indications about the statements in this book concerning the poor. They are in all cases people who are materially poor. I regard Gelin's spiritualizing interpretation as incorrect.

The precondition of Zephaniah's appearance (here he does not differ from the pre-exilic prophets) was that Israel had long since fallen from the condition of wholeness in which Yahweh had placed it at the beginning of its history. This state of things evoked the prophetic proclamation of judgment which proved itself valid, step by step, in the course of history. But very early, beginning with Elijah, we find, even in the prophets of disaster, the beginning of hope. Should the present Israel perish because of its backsliding from the work that Yahweh had planned for it—nevertheless, Yahweh will not abandon those whom he once rescued from misery. The remnant will be saved, and with them Yahweh will make a new beginning. Among these prophets of judgment and of hope for a new beginning with a "remnant," some hundred years after the Jerusalem prophet Isaiah, we now find Zephaniah. He is the first to name this "remnant" that is to be saved in order to begin anew more concretely as "the poor."

Equally important for understanding Zephaniah is another prophetic tradition—the saying about the "day of Yahweh." In its original form, going back before the writing prophets, it probably said that all the nations in this world, which is rotten to its roots, are heading for destruction. The "day of Yahweh" is this end; God himself will descend upon the nations and put an end to all of them. Coupled with this is the idea that then Israel, Yahweh's new and different society, will stand shining forth. But Amos of Tekoa had already turned this view of things on its head. Israel has deserted its task, and Israel must also reckon with the "day of Yahweh." The book of Zephaniah takes up this theme. But there it is again turned upside down. Let us look at it in detail!

The first section (1:2 - 2:3) says that the day of Yahweh will come upon the whole creation, but especially Jerusalem and Judah. Only in the margin, as it were, is there a note on the "poor in the land" who "live according to the law of Yahweh." They are to remain in their paths of righteousness and humble poverty of spirit—perhaps they may be saved (2:3)?

After this proclamation of Yahweh's wrath, the second section (2:4 - 3:7) describes the storm of that wrath. Yahweh has already begun the destruction of the nations, starting with the Gentiles, in order that Jerusalem may see what is happening and perhaps may repent. But nothing of the sort happens. The last chance for repentance is missed (3:6-7).

The subject of the third section is then Yahweh's definitive action (3:8-15)—and here we find the great surprise and thereby the individual statement of the book. Yahweh's final act will be entirely different from what one would expect after the first two sections. The saying about the "day of Yahweh" will be reversed once more. With expressions that traditionally invite confidence, Zephaniah encourages his hearers to look forward to the day when Yahweh will appear accuser. Yahweh would have the right to gather nations and assemble kingdoms in order to pour out his fury, indeed the whole heat of his anger on them: "For in the fire of my jealous wrath all the earth should be consumed"(3:8). But he will not give rein to his anger. He will do something entirely different:

> I will change the lips of the peoples into lips that are clean, that all of them may call on the name of Yahweh and serve him shoulder to shoulder. From beyond the rivers of Africa they will bring me offerings. (3:9-10)

In the midst of the destroying judgment, perhaps even in place of destruction, God has thus worked a miracle of conversion, not on Israel, but on the Gentiles. A pilgrimage of the nations to Jerusalem begins. What do they find there?

Jerusalem should have been put to deepest shame because of its misdeeds. But when the nations begin their pilgrimage to Jerusalem, Yahweh takes away its reason for shame (3:11a). "Then I will remove from your midst your proud boasters, and you shall no longer be haughty on my holy mountain" (3:11b). And now comes the decisive statement. The newly-restored Jerusalem is a Jerusalem of the poor:

> I leave in the midst of you as a rescued remnant a people humble and poor.
>
> They will seek refuge in the name of Yahweh—this remnant of Israel.
>
> They will do no wrong and utter no lies, nor shall there be found in their mouth a deceitful tongue.
>
> No, they shall pasture and lie down, and none shall make them afraid. (3:12-13)

Then begins the hymn which closes the original book:

> Sing aloud, O daughter of Zion; shout, O Jerusalem!
>
> Rejoice and exult with all your heart!
>
> Yahweh has taken away the judgments against you, He has converted your enemy.
>
> Yahweh is in your midst as king of Israel.
>
> You shall fear evil no more. (3:14-15)

The day of Yahweh will thus, in the end, be salvation and not destruction. But this in no way justifies the deterioration of the Yahweh-society. Yahweh will cause his salvation to bypass his original chosen people and begin in the pagan world. He will then lead these nations in a pilgrimage to Jerusalem. And then, in this context, salvation will return to Jerusalem. But it will be represented there not by the upper classes who in their pride have brought Jerusalem to destruction; instead, it will be there in the persons of their previous victims, the poor. The new Jerusalem will be a city of the poor of Yahweh.

A lot more could be said about the book of Zephaniah, and it would be especially interesting to show how the astonishing statement in part three was already concealed in what went before. But I will drop the discussion of Zephaniah at this point. It has served to show where and in what context the perspective shifts from a look backward at a rescue of the poor at the beginning of Israel's history to a look forward into the future, where for the first time the theme of God's concern for the poor appears as the coming hope of Israel.

Even in this first appearance, we find it in a horizon that embraces all the societies of the earth. But it is just as clear that it is not a matter of just any poor people, nor of all the world's poor, but of those children of the people Israel who are again what all the children of Israel were at the beginning of their history—poor and exploited. But now they are the poor and exploited within Israel itself.

All these motifs and motif complexes were already developed and available to Deutero-Isaiah when, at a point still farther along the historical continuum, after the destruction of Jerusalem and the deportation to Babylon, he conceived his incomparable oratorio of consolation and hope.

The Gospel for the Poor in Deutero- and Trito-Isaiah

Deutero-Isaiah presupposes that the transformation of the day of Yahweh into its contrary (namely the new possibility of salvation), proposed as a vision in the book of Zephaniah, is something that is happening at the present moment. He also sees better than Zephaniah (who gives no reason for God's change of heart), and perhaps under the influence of Habbakuk, why God suddenly changes his mind. First, Israel fell victim to Yahweh's wrath and thereby became poor. It became the nation of the "poor of Yahweh" because Yahweh himself made it poor. But then the other nations, Yahweh's instruments of punishment, overstepped their duty and have themselves committed excesses. They have treated Israel unjustly. So Israel has become the nation of the "poor of Yahweh" in a second and unique sense; namely, a suffering people whom he joins to himself once more in solidarity (cf. 42:18-25; 51:17-23; 47:6-9).

In contrast to Zephaniah, Deutero-Isaiah does not speak of the poor in Israel, but rather of all Israel as the poor of Yahweh. One could explain that, of course, by saying that now, after judgment has fallen on Israel, only a poor remnant survives, and this remnant is all that is left of Israel. This is certainly accurate, for it corresponds to the changed situation out of which Deutero-Isaiah is writing. But at the same time, this tension between the different relationships of the "poor" to Israel as a whole—as part or as all of Israel—is present from this point onward and remains relevant.

In the Isaiah 40-55, the term "poor" appears in only five places: 41:17; 49:13; 51:21; 54:11,14. But this is partly a result of the image-laden and concrete language of Deutero-Isaiah. He always portrays things as individually and graphically as possible. In reality, one can regard long passages in Deutero-Isaiah as statements on the "poor of Yahweh." These texts can be divided into two groups, depending on whether the view is directed toward the people remaining in the land or toward those deported and enslaved in Babylon. When the text has in mind the people in Judah, Zion-Jerusalem usually appears in the shape of a poor and miserable woman. If it looks to Babylon, we ordinarily find the masculine persona of the servant of Yahweh. This play on symbolic figures of differing sex in the same text had already been skillfully developed by the young Jeremiah in the original text of Jeremiah 30-31. In Deutero-Isaiah the figure of the servant of God dominates the first half of the text, the figure of Zion-Jerusalem the second half; but it is a matter of predominance, not of exclusivity. The two perspectives blend in two places, at the point where Deutero-Isaiah announces the return of the exiles and the reconstitution of Israel in Jerusalem.

In connection with the return of the poor deportees, which is mainly portrayed in terms of a march accompanied by miraculous events through a desert which has been transformed into a garden, the Exodus theme is frequently suggested. The old Exodus at the beginning of Israel's history will be mirrored in a new Exodus when Yahweh brings Israel home and establishes his society in Jerusalem anew.

I can here only give a global overview of these rich and many-sided texts. There is little point in giving a long list of citations. But I want to say expressly that I would include the so-called suffering servant songs in such a list. One brief remark: I personally consider the theory that four originally independent "suffering servant songs" which, according to most proponents of the theory, speak of an individual prophet or king, have been secondarily introduced into the text of Isaiah 40-55 to be unproven. In fact, the theory appears to me to be false. For if one removes these four songs from the text, it collapses for want of many of its supporting pillars. What remains is an unconnected chaos of individual text fragments. That is why the newer commentaries often have such a hard time with the interpretation of Deutero-Isaiah. They can say a great deal about individual details but little about the book as a whole. As parts of the whole, these four so-called suffering servant songs clearly have a collective sense and refer to Israel in exile, impoverished and humiliated, tortured even to destruction. This is my own interpretation, which I have documented more fully in a published essay (*Festschrift for J. Ziegler*). However, if anyone is absolutely convinced that these four texts existed separately and with individual reference before the composition of the present complete text of Isaiah 40-55, I would consider that admissible, provided she or he admits that later, through their inclusion in the present context, the texts were given a collective meaning. In what follows, I am concerned only with the completed text of Deutero-Isaiah, not its extremely hypothetical pre-history. The later "messianic" interpretation of these texts, which necessarily referred them to an individual, poses no problem as far as I am concerned. Even if the individual texts of Deutero-Isaiah or its complete text are to be read as collective reference to Israel, they could be applied to the Messiah as an individual in a context of messianic expectation. For Jesus is the fulfillment of everything that is promised of "Israel." He is Israel personified, and for that very reason he is the Messiah.

Unfortunately, it would be quite impossible to cite and comment on the many beautiful texts in Deutero-Isaiah concerning the "poor of Yahweh." I can only summarize the principal points that are relevant to our question:

• Again, as in the original Exodus and later in Zephaniah, it is
a question of genuine poor people. These include both the
Israelites who were deported to Babylon and those who
remained behind in Judah. Even if individual families suc-
ceeded in recovering a measure of well-being in Babylon, still
they were all there as exiles in a foreign land. Their freedom
of movement was limited. They were in all respects dependent
on their foreign surroundings, and all Jerusalem was a ruin,
already generations old. There was no real governing class, for
they were in Babylon. The government officials to whom
Judah was subject lived in despised Samaria and returned hate
for hate.

• Again, as in the original Exodus, the promises in Deutero-
Isaiah concern the action of Yahweh alone. Everything that is
promised has the character of a miracle through and through,
and with what miraculous colors is the return home through
the blossoming desert depicted!

• Again, as in the first Exodus, it is to be the beginning of a new
society that human beings themselves could not achieve, in
which only plenty and happiness determine the human lot,
and there is no longer a difference between rich and poor.
Yahweh will bring Israel once more into its land, and it will
live as Yahweh's society. This is expressed primarily in the
image of the new Jerusalem, founded on jewels and built of
precious stones. All its inhabitants learn Yahweh's Torah and
therefore they live together in peace and justice (cf. 54:11-14).

• Different, on the other hand, from the first Exodus is the
subject of the whole event. The "poor of Yahweh" are no
longer just any poor people; they are the people of God who
have been thrust into misery by the nations. This people is
trapped in the guilt of its own failure, and to that extent it is
bearing the consequences of its own deeds. God is turning to
those poor people who have destroyed his own plan for human
history. They would not be poor if they had listened to him.

They had been his hope. But at the same time these are the people God loves, a multitude marked with an indelible sign. Their overlords, the nations and the kings of the world, recognize this too, and that is why they oppress these peo - ple—because they are the unique nation in world history, the people marked by Yahweh as his own.

* This history of God with his poor takes place also on a new, worldwide stage. It is no longer a single state that exploits the poor in its own land, poor people made such by the system and making up part of that system. In Deutero-Isaiah, as already in Zephaniah, the whole human world is the horizon of the vision. What is new is that now the poor themselves are defined in light of the whole, and not of a partial society. The basic opposition in Deutero-Isaiah is that between Israel and its God on the one hand, the nations and their gods on the other. The whole world system appears as a single structure of abasement and oppression. Its victim is Yahweh's servant who, however, in the midst of every chastisement that strikes him, can always be sure that Yahweh is on his side. He is, despite his failure, at the same time one who listens with his whole attention, like a child who is being taught, and who speaks with the tongue of one who is taught. Therefore, he is persecuted by the nations and he does not resist, but gives his back to the smiters (50:4-6). Yahweh himself lets him become the place where the iniquity of the whole world is concen - trated (53:8-9). In a collective reading of the persona of the servant of God, this can only mean that everything ends with the destruction of Israel as a social reality, and for the individ - ual Israelite with his or her own death or at least with the loss of personal identity. To phrase this with an eye to the Gospel texts of the New Testament, here the poverty of Israel is connected to its persecution for God's sake and for the sake of justice. Not just any group of poor people, even though God might intend something new and great with them, but this particular group of poor people within the world horizon, who are the object of the care and concern of the true God and who for that reason are humbled and persecuted—these are the object of God's "option for the poor." He chooses

those who have already had a long relationship with Him and
therefore are being persecuted for His sake. In that sense they
are "His poor."

- The rescue of the people of God from its poverty of persecution is thus not a simple Exodus. The world as such is changed
  as a result. God's instrument for the salvation of Israel is
  created out of the midst of the other nations—Cyrus, who is
  even given the title "Yahweh's Messiah" (45:1). The nations
  of the world are also abandoned by their own gods, who show
  themselves to be non-existent (41:29; 45:5 among many other
  places). Babylon, the typical power of the oppressive world
  system, collapses (46-47). The nations recognize that Jerusalem is the center of the world, that its God is the only one, and
  they set out on pilgrimage to Jerusalem (45:14; 52:13-15).

Yahweh's plan is now more comprehensive than in the first
Exodus. If at that time he planned to constitute, at last, a just people
in contrast to the other nations, this time he makes the nation created
out of his poor to be a model for all societies. He makes it the center,
the point of attraction, for all the nations. Israel will be his "witness,"
and a light for the nations, the bringer of justice (42:3-4,6; 49:6;
51:4-5; 55:4-5). In the end, the reconstitution of the Yahweh-society
out of poor and persecuted Israel promotes the transformation of the
whole of world society.

All this is proclamation. It breathes expectance. But still it is only
a messenger of good tidings announcing the gospel. The promised
fulfillment is not yet at hand.

When did all this become reality? Clearly, though a part of the
deported people returned home, the Temple in Jerusalem was rebuilt
from its ruins, and a new polity was begun. Still, the radiant fullness
of all that was promised in this "gospel" was far from being accom -
plished. So the prophetic word points to a more distant future.

The Path of the Gospel for the Poor through the Old Testament

The gospel of Deutero-Isaiah was repeatedly reformulated in the sequel as a forward-looking promise, especially in those still later chapters that were added to the book of Isaiah, which we call Trito-Isaiah.

The central text of Trito-Isaiah is found in chapters 60-62. Its language imitates Deutero-Isaiah, and much of it is simply a midrash on texts from Deutero-Isaiah. The portrait of the future is even more colorful and dazzling, especially the pilgrimage of the nations to Zion. This eschatological event will mark a turning point from poverty to wealth, as well as the advent of peace and of just dealing with one another. Here again all Israelites form the group of the poor and oppressed (especially in 61:1-7).

But one thing that belonged to the core of the message in Deutero-Isaiah does not reappear so clearly—that the whole change is brought about through the suffering and death of God's servant. To the extent that this is no longer present, we also lose the feeling that God's action is not only impending but already present, even if one experiences at first only its suffering aspect. The present epoch thus becomes a kind of empty period of waiting, and the fulfillment recedes into the distance. But since these texts and others that were added still later could scarcely have existed independently of the book of Isaiah, we have to wonder whether readers of Deutero-Isaiah were consciously aware of the difference.

The influence of the whole book of Isaiah (whose tone as a completed whole was certainly determined primarily by Deutero-Isaiah) on the thought of the Jewish people in the last centuries before Christ can hardly be underestimated. The book also provided a kind of hermeneutical key to the praying of the psalter, at least insofar as the psalms present themselves as prayers of "the poor."

One of the sources for the suffering servant of Yahweh, this figure of Israel in Deutero-Isaiah, was certainly Israel's collection of personal songs of lament. In many of them, those lamenting say that they are persecuted and oppressed by other people, whether deserv - edly or without personal guilt. In their distress, they turn to their God. They do not accept the projections their persecuters impose on them; instead, they trust that Yahweh is on their side, the side of the persecuted poor. In this confidence, the poor person who is praying recognizes the true God as he really is—the one who pities and rescues the poor. This is the very perception that has become, in Deutero-Isaiah, the core of Israel's hope for salvation: That Yahweh reveals the truth about himself in the very suffering and death of the poor and brings them salvation. This original connection between songs of lament and the message of the suffering servant of God could now be reversed, from the perspective of Deutero-Isaiah, and be used to shed light on the individual laments in the Psalms. These were especially appropriate to the purpose since the poor persons who speak them could be seen as personifications of Israel, the poor people of God, living among the hostile nations of the world as the persecuted and oppressed society of Yahweh and waiting for Yahweh's salvation. The individual could experience himself or herself as a member of this Israel, "collectively" understood, which prays the psalms.

This hermeneutic must have been so powerful that it often led to the addition of verses at the ends of the psalms which reinterpreted them to make them fit (cf. for example Psalm 22 or 69) and even to new poetic compositions in which statements about the poor as individuals and as all of Israel are arranged side by side and are interwoven (cf. for example Psalm 102). Besides the psalms in which the persons praying refer to themselves explicitly as poor, others which concern the persecution or illness of those praying were also undoubtedly understood in a similar collective sense.

An impressive witness to this hermeneutic is the great commentary on Psalm 37 from the Qumran caves, in which everything in the Psalm is interpreted as referring to the Qumran community as the true Israel under persecution by its enemies.

I will break off the discussion of the Old Testament texts at this point in order to finish this chapter with a concluding section concerning the New Testament.

The "Poor of Yahweh" in the New Testament

There can be no doubt that Jesus took up this concept of the "poor of Yahweh." It would be absolutely contrary to the way in which he referred to Isaiah in what he said and did, especially in his many works of healing, if one were to perceive him as preaching a gospel for all the poor of the world.

This is not to say that God's action in and for "his poor," namely for Israel, the persecuted victim of the nations, should not be expected to have universal consequences in precisely the sense indicated in the book of Isaiah. Clearly, Deutero-Isaiah already sees everything against a universal horizon, and God's intention is not merely the restoration of Israel, but the transformation of the whole human society. But "his poor," in whose salvation from death he wills to begin this eschatological world process, are some very particular "poor" among all the poor of the world. They are his Israel. In and through the fact that this Israel is saved and transformed into a new society in which there are no differences between rich and poor, upper and lower, ruler and ruled, the whole of human society is to be enabled to join this movement and to eliminate poverty every - where.

But human society is not deprived of its freedom. It can still say no. And it did say no. The Gospels portray the drama as, on the one side, the new life blossomed around Jesus, while, on the other side, the old society hardened its heart, persecuted and finally killed God's righteous one. That was not the end. God raised his servant from death, and his work continued, so that the jaws of the netherworld can never devour it. The new society arising out of Jesus' gospel for the poor is in the world now. Long ago it broke through the bounds of the original Israel, and the pilgrimage of the nations has been in progress ever since. But its history remains marked even today by the paradox of the fate of the servant of God: Salvation comes only in and through persecution. In other words, where the gospel for Yahweh's poor truly prevails, the transformation of this world really happens. To everyone's astonishment, there comes into being the miracle of a society in which people can relate in a new way to material things and to one another and where, as a result, there is no more poverty. But in the same measure as the members of this society experience the abolition of every kind of poverty, they also discover how the old society closes ranks against them and begins to persecute them. And the odd thing is that both of these experiences belong together and are intimately connected—that of the miracle of the abolition of poverty and at the same time that of being thrown back again into the poverty of persecution.

This is the deeper logic of the beatitudes, whether one reads them in Matthew's version (Matt 5:3-12) or in Luke's (Luke 6:20-23). First the poor are declared blessed—in Matthew, as well, it is not only those with an inner commitment to poverty, but (despite an often-cited parallel from Qumran) really poor people—those, how - ever, in whom the Spirit of God from Isa 61:1 has already begun to work. The poor, the hungry, those who mourn, those who thirst for a more just society are called blessed and the reign of God, now perceptively beginning, is to be theirs. Theirs is the new, different society. But this is immediately followed by the blessing of those who are to be persecuted for this new way of life, here called "righteousness."

This messianic proto-paradox—that poverty will be abolished and at the same time will return in the form of a poverty of persecution, and that both realities go together—should presumably be kept in mind also in order to understand correctly Jesus' depiction of the judgment of the world in Matthew 25, at least in its basic message, not as later interpreted for purposes of Christian parenesis. Its background is the question asked by Jesus' followers: How can those who have not followed the Messiah be saved, those who may know nothing of him, who perhaps are even tempted to persecute us? It is not a matter of the salvation of Christians. They are saved by following Jesus. It is a question of the rest of human society, the "nations" in Old Testament terminology, those who do not belong to the "least of these" (another term for Yahweh's poor). God's attitude to them is determined by their attitude to the poor—concretely: to the hungry, the thirsty, strangers, the naked, the sick, the prisoners. But these are not just any of the poor of this world. They are those "poor" in whom the Son of Man, (the Human One), the new society of God, is present. In view of this, the judge's answer is unambiguous, and it is amazing that so often no one seems to catch it: These are "the least of these, my sisters and brothers." This is usually interpreted as if Jesus were identifying himself with all the world's poor. But from the linguistic usage of Matthew's gospel, which is normally very precise, that can scarcely be the original meaning. It is a matter of the poor of Yahweh, the poor who have come to Jesus and have entered with him into the reign of God. The nations are spontaneously determined to persecute them because they are different. If they do not, but instead are overcome with sympathy, it is as if they themselves have already entered into the reign of God, simply because they were kind. To formulate this as a principle: The Israelites themselves will be judged by whether they have eliminated poverty in Israel by following Jesus and acting accordingly. The "nations," that is, those who do not belong to God's kingdom, or at least not yet, will be judged by their conduct toward the "poor of Yahweh," when they meet them in the flesh and in their need. One need not necessarily have entered into the kingdom of God in order to receive eternal life. For those who have not, it is enough to have had pity of the "poor of the kingdom" and not to have joined their persecutors.

This is a very different interpretation of Matthew 25 from what one finds in the work of the theologians of liberation. Next to the Exodus story, Matthew 25 is probably the biblical text most often cited by them. It is read in reference to all the poor of the world, and it follows that every poor person in the world is seen as a kind of epiphany of Christ. An exegete feels almost like an oppressor of the poor, one who takes their holiest dignity from them if it seems necessary for exegetical reasons to defend another interpretation like the one just given. Nevertheless, it appears to me to be the only correct one, at least as far as the basic form of the story is concerned.

However, if rightly regarded, it takes nothing at all away from the poor in our world.

For one thing, the Latin-American theologians of liberation themselves continually assure us that their continent is a Christian one and not, like Europe or North America, a region that has returned to paganism. And they may well be right. I cannot explain the unbelievable dynamism of the basic community movement in that continent in any other way. The poor there thus belong to those "least of all," to "Yahweh's poor" in whom the Messiah really is manifest when they listen to his gospel for the poor.

Secondly, as we saw in the first chapter, it is our duty, quite apart from what is distinctively biblical, to develop an ethic of concern for the poor. This would already give us appropriate reason to do most of what the theologians of liberation demand of us, and it is in this area alone that one can dialogue with all people of good will.

It is another question whether on this level the liberation of the poor that God has in mind will really last and not result in just another game of musical chairs among different elite groups. Unless every - thing I have said to this point is false, God's plan for the transforma- tion of the world proceeds by means of a contrast-people. But one can enter this new society only by following Jesus. There is no cheap route divorced from faith. Anyone who interprets the central texts of the Bible concerning the poor as meaning some kind of aid for the poor that is possible without faith and without transformation of the world within the believing community is misusing these texts and is not doing them justice.

I am not saying that the liberation theologians do that. But they are struggling. Their great advantage is that the growing basic com - munities interpret the fundamental message of the Bible for them in a kind of continual renewal based on reality. They need only accept what the Spirit of God is doing before their very eyes for the real and enduring benefit of the poor. In this sense God himself, working in history, is coming to the theologian's aid. If they continue to have difficulties, then we biblical scholars may have to ask ourselves whether we have done too little to interpret the Bible for them. That is a serious question, and one I often ask myself.

Other Titles Available from BIBAL Press